NOON

NOON

GOD'S HOURLY, DAILY AND
MONTHLY BLESSINGS

HENRY WALKER

TATE PUBLISHING & *Enterprises*

Published by Tate Publishing & Enterprises, LLC
127 E. Trade Center Terrace | Mustang, Oklahoma 73064 USA
1.888.361.9473 | www.tatepublishing.com

Tate Publishing is committed to excellence in the publishing industry. The company reflects the philosophy established by the founders, based on Psalm 68:11,
"The Lord gave the word and great was the company of those who published it."

Book design copyright © 2009 by Tate Publishing, LLC. All rights reserved.
Cover design by Kandi Evans
Interior design by Joey Garrett

Published in the United States of America

ISBN: 978-1-60799-254-7
1. Religion / Prayer
2. Religion / Meditations
11.09.12

DEDICATION

This book is dedicated to my Lord Jesus, who gave me the inspiration, wisdom, and anointing to write this book and to my wife Breda, who is always there for me. She encourages me so very much.

ACKNOWLEDGMENTS

I really appreciate my friend William, who has encouraged and helped me for years. He is a man of great integrity and honesty, and he is a very special friend.

TABLE OF CONTENTS

INTRODUCTION

This book is the sequel to *Seasons: God's Timing for Special Blessings*. In preparing to write *Seasons,* God revealed to me the knowledge of his weekly and seasonal blessings.

However, when I was preparing for this book, God also revealed that there are certain hours of the day that are reserved for special blessings. In addition, he revealed to me that that there are special blessings in every month as a whole in addition to certain unique blessings on particular days of each month. Surely, he can bless at any time, but he has reserved certain times of the day, as well as certain days of the month and certain months as a whole, for special, unique blessings. These are special times which he anoints to bring about miracles, and our job is to be aware of these times in order to receive the blessings.

There is a special anointing by God for us to accomplish specific things in our lives at certain times of the year. It is our responsibility to let him prepare us for these special times and to know what to expect when those particular times arrive. If you don't receive the blessing that you are expecting at a certain period of time, maybe God is trying to make some adjustments in your life, in order for you to receive. Just listen to the Holy Spirit and believe to receive at the next time period.

You will be so filled with joy as you learn of his special blessing times and how much he wants to bless us, his children. He is working so hard to let us know when and how he wants to pour out blessings that we won't have room enough to contain. The first time of the day I want to discuss is the Noon Time Blessing.

Before I start, one thing that we have to realize is that according to the Word (Leviticus 23:32) our twenty-four-hour period of time which includes day and night both starts and ends at evening (6:00 P.M.). Within this twenty-four-hour period of time, there are four evening watches – 6:00 P.M.-9:00 P.M., 9: 00 P.M.-12:00 A.M., 12:00 A.M.-3:00 A.M., and 3:00 A.M.-6:00 A.M. These intimate evening watches with the Lord which prepare us for the daily hourly blessings, are explained later on in the book. Also, within this twenty-four-hour period of time, 6:00 A.M. marks the first hour of the daytime and runs to 7:00 A.M., so 7: 00 A.M. is the end of the first hour of the day. The end of the third hour of the day is 9:00 A.M. and this hour runs from 8:00 A.M. to 9:00 A.M. The end of the sixth hour of the day is 12:00 P.M. and this hour runs from 11:00 A.M. to 12:00 P.M., and so forth. The daytime ends at 6:00 P.M., and the evening watches start. The hourly blessings that we will be talking about occur exactly at the end of the third, sixth, seventh, ninth, eleventh hours of the day, as well as Midnight (9:00 A.M., 12:00 P.M., 1:00 P.M., 3:00 P.M., 5:00 P.M. and Midnight). The hour preceding the blessed time is when God is preparing you for the blessing, and the devil may be trying to distract you from the blessing. For example, God may want to bless you at the third hour of the day (9:00 A.M.). At 8:00 A.M. God is moving to prepare you for this blessing, and the devil wants to distract you to miss the third hour blessing that will occur at exactly 9:00 A.M.

The particular blessings that are attached to a certain hour of time correlate with the various time zones people are in. God is powerful enough to move uniquely on anyone's time zone. Start praying and preparing for these blessings in advance. The way to prepare for these blessings is to allow God to mortify the deeds of your flesh daily (Romans 8:13) and continue to allow God to change you into the image of Jesus. You cannot receive the blessings that are outlined in this book without doing so.

We need to start basing our spiritual walk with Jesus on the Hebrew calendar, in order to be on his time-table. As a result, I have prepared charts at the end of the book to point out to you when the monthly periods start on our Gregorian calendar as compared to the biblical or Hebrew calendar for the years 2010–2012. I have also done the same for God's feasts days for the same period of time. In order to see dates beyond 2012, you can go to my Web site at www.henrywalker.org and click on *Biblical Calendar*. Please use www.hebcal.com/hebcal in conjunction with my site (or another site with a Hebrew calendar) to find out when a particular day on the Hebrew calendar falls on the Gregorian calendar. When you are on this Web site please check off "show Hebrew date for entire date range" under "Other Options." Please remember that the twenty-four-hour period of time which includes day and night runs from evening to evening. Remember that God works on his calendar, which is the Hebrew, or biblical, calendar.

THE HOUR OF POWER

God deals with us in hourly intervals at times. In a particular hour that God moves, you can feel him prompting you in the spirit. He wants to do something special for you at that actual hour, and he is truly moving on the scene to do so.

In 1 Peter 1:6–7, Paul says to rejoice if you are going through trials and temptations because Jesus Christ will appear on the scene to help you. So you may be going through something bad, but God is alerting you to the fact that he is now moving on your behalf during a particular hour of the day. What the enemy tries to do, if allowed, is follow what Jesus is doing and try to distort this particular hour of blessing. What he tries to do is distract you from God's presence and get you to focus on some problem he is setting up. He is hoping that you miss what God is trying to do in your life by taking away your expectation. Satan hopes that you will put all your attention on his circumstance. He wants you to think that *he* controls this hour and not God.

Satan doesn't act with sovereignty. He works for God! He tried to rebel against God, but God subdued him and cast him out of heaven to the earth. He is controlled by God. God gives him his assignments. When Satan approached God as recorded in the book of Job, it was God who suggests Job. He said, "Have you considered my servant Job?" He gave Satan the assignment to test Job. All Satan was doing was coming to the boss and getting his next assignment!

God controls everything and everybody. All things were created by Jesus and for Jesus, and by him all things consist (Colossians 1:16–17). So, God controls Satan. He has no power unless God gives it to him.

In Revelation 3:10, Jesus talks about the hour of temptation. As I mentioned before, God chooses an hour to bless you, and the devil may try to invade that hour to make it his hour of temptation. This is evident in the third chapter of Daniel. In verse 6, King Nebuchadnezzar says that if anyone in the kingdom refuses to worship the image he set up, that person will be killed in the same hour. In verse 13, the king arrests the three Hebrew children (who refused to worship the pagan image), so this hour of time has now started! As we know from verses 29 and 30, the Hebrew children got promoted, so could it be that God ordained this hour? God chose an hour to bless the children and was only using Nebuchadnezzar to set up the whole event. Nebuchadnezzar throws them into the fiery furnace, and they are not harmed, even though the king turns the fire up seven times hotter.

God set up this event to show his power and to promote the Hebrew children. God controlled the hour and actually *chose* that very hour to bless those children! The hour of God's blessing the three children ended when the king made a decree in verse 29 that everybody should worship the God of the Hebrew children. Also, at the end of the hour, he also promoted the children as recorded in verse 30, which is just what God wanted to do during this hour.

So you see, God has reserved hourly blessings for his people. Again, as he starts prompting you in your spirit, be aware and expect him to bless you at the end of that hour. Also, don't be surprised if the devil tries to distract you from what God is doing. The Word says in

Revelation 8:1 that there was silence in heaven for half an hour. So when the devil is trying to distract you during the hour that God is moving, keep quiet for half an hour, worship God during the remaining half hour, and then expect the blessing at the end of the hour!

Please remember in the succeeding chapters that God wants to move during that hour to change your life. Please expect it and allow him to do so. But again, don't let the devil distract you during that hour.

NOON TIME BLESSING

(Sixth Hour of the Day)

Remember that the main requirement to receive these hourly blessings, or any blessing from God, is to allow him to continue to change us into the image of Jesus. This is imperative! God is always interested in the spiritual blessings first. "Seek ye first the kingdom of God and his righteousness; and all these things shall be added unto you" (Matthew 6:33).

I want to start with the noon time blessing because God has shown me more about this hour than any other hour of the day. The noon time blessing happens exactly at noon. The first indication of this blessing is recorded in Genesis 43 in the story of Joseph. His brothers come to him for food, and he recognizes them, but they don't recognize him. He sends them back to bring their youngest brother, Benjamin. He also puts the money they paid him in their sacks as they leave. They get back to Jacob, their father, and he tells them to take Benjamin to Joseph and take double the money and other presents for Joseph. When they get to Joseph, they present the gift to Joseph at noon as they eat together (verses 25–26). There is a great anointing on this hour to receive a blessing through the very same people who want to hurt you. As you know, the brothers are the ones who turn Joseph over to slavery.

It doesn't matter what plans your enemies have against you and what they might have already tried. God has anointed the noon time for you to receive unexpected blessings through such people. They are being forced to do this because God has given you authority over them. You are now the head; they are the tail. You are now above; they are below. God has reversed the tables. He has given you the advantage. All Joseph has to do is forgive his brothers and treat them nicely. This was an unexpected blessing and one that he didn't even need. The same thing could happen to you. Just start preparing at the beginning of the day, which is sundown for this special noon time blessing that can occur.

Another thing that happens in this story is that Joseph and his brothers sit together and no Egyptian sits near them. There is a separation anointing at this time, and God could be starting to pull people out of your life. This separation could start with a noon day phone call, where somebody in your life says he or she is moving to another location. You just have to realize that there is a separation anointing on this hour to help you achieve your purpose by removing people from your life who are obstacles. You have to be willing to let them go.

This separation anointing could also remove situations out of your way, by finally having them be resolved, in your favor. In my own life, I was working on a situation for over three months and expecting God to give me the victory. Finally, on a particular day at noon, I got the phone call that the situation had been resolved in my favor. Praise God! At that time, God had just started dealing with me about this noon time blessing. He really demonstrated this truth. Whatever is coming against you and is nagging at your mind, release it to God, and expect at every noon time for it to be resolved in your favor until it is.

You can also expect God to separate you from the

things that are coming between you and him (i.e. hidden sins and sinful habits). Just tell God that your number one prayer is for him to conform you to the image of Jesus. The Word says in Romans 8:13 that only the Spirit of God can "mortify" the deeds of the flesh. Only God can strengthen us enough not to sin. Allow him to separate you from your sins and fleshly desires. All we can do is make a quality decision that we don't want to sin and by his power, especially at noon time, he can remove the power of these sins from your life once and for all. Praise him!

Another thing that happened in the Joseph story is that, by an act of God, all the brothers sit at the table in the order of their birthright. This is truly amazing! There is such an anointing at this time to bring order to your family. At a particular noon time, he can start the process of bringing order into the lives of your loved ones. You might get a phone call from a runaway son or daughter at noon time and hear that he or she wants to come home. There is no telling what God can do. All you have to do is prepare and expect. You may get a phone call from your spouse that he or she was just born again. He can start to bring order out of a family trial at noon time, no matter how long it has been going on.

Joseph gives the youngest brother, Benjamin, five times as much as the others. There is such an anointing on this time to bless the least likely (i.e. to make the last to be first). You may feel that you are the least likely to be blessed, but there is an anointing on this hour to prove you wrong. Just think about David, the least likely in the eyes of man but chosen by God to be king. God loves to raise up the underdog. Just maintain your humility with God's help and watch what he does for you.

This noon meal with Joseph also puts into motion

abundance for all the brothers. In Genesis 44:1, after their meal, Joseph tells his servants to fill his brothers' sacks with food and return their money in the same sacks. This is a time for God to put into motion a blessing that costs you nothing, an abundance. Just allow God to prepare you and cleanse you by the Word, and watch his anointing for abundance to start working in your life.

This meal also triggers the event where Joseph reveals his identity to his brothers. There is an anointing on the noon time hour for Jesus, who is our brother, as well as our God, to reveal more about himself to us. We find out more of what he really is like as he draws us closer to him, especially at noon.

In 2 Samuel chapter 4, there is another revelation about this blessing. In verses 5–7, it is recorded that two men kill one of the main enemies of King David at noon. As I mentioned earlier, God can separate people from your life (I don't mean kill them), but here he shows that he can use somebody else to move them out of your life. Wow! He really is awesome.

Remember in Judges 3 how God uses a man named Ehud to secretly kill the enemy king who had kept them in bondage for eighteen years (verse 21). God uses one man to rescue a whole nation. Get ready for God to use others to separate you from situations and people, starting at noon.

Another example of this blessing is contained in 1 Kings 18:19–40. Here Elijah challenges 850 false prophets in front of all Israel. He challenges them to call upon their God to burn up a sacrifice, a bullock. At noon, they start to call upon their God (Baal) until the evening sacrifice (3:00 P.M.), but to no avail. God has the devil bound up. This is evident because in the book of Revelation, the False Prophet will call down fire from heaven. God has bound Baal. God starts binding the devil from certain areas of your life at this time. Praise him!

This time period (12:00 P.M. to 3:00 P.M.) is a great time wherever possible to schedule meetings on important issues because the devil is bound. You will find that the meetings will go smoother. If you are being attacked and there is a meeting that has been arranged against you between these hours, you need to rejoice. Go into the meeting confident that you have the victory already in hand because the devil is bound! Of course, God can give you victory at any time of day, but there is a special anointing on this time period.

At this same event (Elijah and the false prophets), God does send down fire from heaven and burn up the sacrifice, along with the altar. God shows up for Elijah, starting at noon, and he will do the same for you. He wants to show up when you are being challenged for him. If you feel that you are being closed in by circumstances or people, allow God to rise to the challenge, starting at noon.

David mentions how he prays to God at noon in Psalm 55:17, and he delivered David from his enemies (verse 18). The event concerning Elijah and the false prophets also starts rain after a three-and-a-half-year drought (1 Kings 18:45). At noon time, he can start raining down blessings on you to let you know that the drought in your life is over.

This event also triggers an enemy in Elijah's life called Jezebel, who God later destroys by the hand of Jehu (2 Kings 9:33). Remember that when God starts blessing, the devil may start messing, but God will take care of him. Just walk in your blessing.

In Song of Solomon 1:7, God says that he makes his

flock to rest at noon. This is a great time just to turn over everything to God and allow him to move on every situation that is coming against you. It is a great time to watch him move as you and I get out of the way. It is such a great time to come into his presence and pour out to him. It is a time set up by him for communion with his children.

During this time, he can tell us how much he loves us and can speak beautiful words of encouragement. Here in verse 9 he compares us to a company of Egyptian horses belonging to Pharaoh. Pharaoh's horses are noted for their swiftness and beauty. In the sight of Christ, his people are the excellence of the earth. It is so great to hear this in his presence, especially if you are tired and under attack. He knows just how to say the right thing to let us know how much he loves us at just the right time. In verses 10–17 he describes our beauty in his sight because of our righteous standing that he gave us and our walk of holiness. He is so happy when his people allow him to sanctify them on a daily basis and conform them into the image of his dear Son.

This noon day rest is so important and confirmed in the book of Hebrews. In Hebrews 4:2, Paul mentions that it takes faith to enter his rest and release situations over to him. It is a matter of ceasing from one's own works (verse 10). It takes work to enter into his rest (verse 10). It may not be easy to get your hands off a situation. God can't move sometimes until you don't. In verse 12 Paul talks about the Word of God being so powerful. This is what happens when we enter that noon time rest. His Word is able to get into the situation and annihilate what is coming against you. So please labor to enter his rest, especially at noon. This rest is for you and I. Enjoy it!

In Isaiah 58:10, God starts talking about some more blessings that can start to occur around the noon time. In verse 10 he talks about bringing his people out of obscurity if they help the hungry and satisfy the afflicted soul. You may have been laboring so long and seen few results and feel that it seems that nobody knows you exist, but this is a time where he can begin to bring you out of obscurity.

Look what he does with David, as recorded in 1 Samuel 16. God sends a prophet by the name of Samuel right to David's house to anoint one of Jesse's sons as king. Wow! That is favor. Samuel looks at every other son that Jesse, the father of David, has and each time God says they are not the one. He finally asks Jesse if he has any other sons. Jesse has to think for a while and remembers David (verse 11).

David is really in obscurity when his father forgets about him. David is the type of person God loves to raise up, (i.e. one who has the odds against him). That description sounds like some of us. Samuel says that nobody will eat until David comes to the table, and Samuel anoints him as king right in the midst of his family. He really takes him out of obscurity. I am sure that when David comes against Goliath, this event is on his mind. God wants to start pouring out favor on your life like he did with David, starting at noon time.

In Isaiah 58:11, another thing is that God will guide us continually and make some adjustments if needed. At noon, if we could just stop from our labors and rest in his presence, he could get us on the right course if need be. How much time and effort his people can save if they allow God to make these adjustments!

In 2 Samuel chapter 5, David is winning battle after battle against the Philistines. He asks God again if he should go against the enemy at Rephaim and if he will win. God tells him to "wait for the sound of the wind coming through the mulberry trees" (verses 22–23). This time he wants David to come behind them. You see, God tells David to rest and instructs him to make a correction in what he is planning to do. God knows he has to make a correction, even though David is having one success after another. He may need to do the same thing with you. Allow him to do so any time he wants, but especially at noon.

In Isaiah 58, God also mentions some other blessings he could start at noon time. When you are going through a dry place, he can "satisfy your soul in drought" (verse 11). He can "make fat your bones," (i.e. start building you up in the Word at this time). He can give you a revelation from the Word that will ignite a fire in you to read his Word without ever wanting to stop.

He also says in verse 11 that we can be like "a watered garden whose waters fail not." He can deposit an anointing in you at this time of day that will never run out. As soon as his anointing goes through to somebody else, as you minister, it will immediately be replenished. Certain ministers won't have to worry about what a ministry trip will cost. God could already have it covered with such a large blessing that the minister won't even think twice about the cost. Praise him! He can start all this at noon. Just get into his presence. It is truly an anointed time.

In verse 12 he mentions that he can bring out an anointing on some people at this time of day to get into people's deepest needs. He mentions that we can "build the old waste places." He can use us to restore hope to people who have no hope and have given up on their dreams. He can ignite a fire in us that will never burn out. He also says we can raise up the foundations of many generations. He can anoint us to teach truths from his Word that can affect generations in families.

Look how God uses Peter in Acts 10. God sends him to Cornelius's house to tell them some new truths. He tells them about Jesus and how he was anointed to destroy the works of the devil (verse 38). As Peter speaks, the Holy Ghost falls on them, and they all are filled with the Spirit (verse 44). We can have this same power.

Also, in Isaiah 58:12, he says we can repair people's lives. We can be spiritual carpenters for Jesus. He can start to bring an anointing out of us to repair people's dreams and lives stronger than they ever were. When a car engine is repaired and rebuilt, it can run better than a new engine. It really depends on the person doing the repairing. God wants to repair his children's lives through us and start bringing out this anointing at noon time. He just loves to start people's lives over. Allow him to bring this anointing out of you.

He also mentions in the same verse that we can restore people's paths. He can use us to give direction to people where there is none. If we desire to help give our kids direction when needed, how much more does our heavenly Father want to do the same with his children?

He also mentions that he can "feed us with the heritage of Jacob." In looking back on the life of Jacob, we can see that God really blesses him. In Genesis 27:28–29 Isaac, his father, pronounces great blessings on him. Among the blessings are: people will serve him and cursed will be everyone who curses him, and blessed will be everyone who blesses him.

In Genesis 28:3–4, his father also says that God will make him fruitful, multiply him, that he will be a multitude of people, and that he and his seed will inherit the land where they are strangers.

In Genesis 48, Joseph brings his two sons, Manasseh and Ephraim, before Jacob, his father, to be blessed. Instead of putting his right hand on Manasseh, the first-born, he puts his right hand on Ephraim, the younger (verse 14). God can put his right hand on you to receive this kind of blessing at this noon time. This is a blessing that others may feel that they should receive, but God has it reserved for you.

In Joshua 16, the tribe of Ephraim receives their inheritance in the new land. In verse 8 the Word says that their "goings out thereof were at the sea." Their inheritance goes out so far that it is beyond their imagination. Because of Jesus, the blessing of Abraham is ours. It is truly an inheritance and because we are Abraham's seed, through Jesus, it is ours.

Jesus was before Abraham (John 8:58). Abraham's blessing flowed right to Ephraim and on to us because of Jesus! Receive the blessing of Ephraim on you right now by faith in Jesus. You need to claim this inheritance, and if your number one prayer is to conform to the image of Jesus, then the benefits of this inheritance are on the way. God is saying that we can be blessed the same way, and it can start at a particular noon time. Wow!

In Jeremiah 6:4, he mentions that noon is a time to declare war. This is also a great time to start an attack on Satan and the strongholds he has on people's lives. This is a great time to intercede and bring down strongholds. Go on the attack.

As I mentioned in my book *Seasons*, the day, according to the Word, our twenty-four-hour period of time which includes day and night both starts and ends at evening (Leviticus 23:32). Please take advantage of this and start your prayers, including warfare prayers, at sundown. Don't wait until the morning. The devil may have already put his plan for you that day into action.

In Matthew 20:5–6, people are called into labor at different hours of the day. People are called into service at the sixth hour (noon). As a result, there is also a great anointing at this hour for God to call people into his service and follow him, at any cost. There is also a great anointing on this hour to give people their assignments (marching orders). This is a revelational period of time for God to give and confirm purpose. If you are not sure about what purpose he has for you, just sit in his presence and soak. He is always willing to communicate, especially at this hour. Please take advantage.

Concerning the sixth hour of the day (noon): in Matthew 27:45, when Jesus is dying, there is darkness from the sixth hour until the ninth hour. Between this time (12 P.M. - 3:00 P.M.), special prayer needs to be made against the kingdom of darkness. The Spirit of God is trying to alert us to these special times of the day. This sixth hour to the ninth hour is a critical time period! We can thwart the plans of darkness during this time! Please intervene in people's lives as the Spirit gives you knowledge. Pull down the strongholds of darkness in their lives.

This time period is also a great time for God to hide you in his presence from any plans the enemy may have. Darkness hides Jesus during this time. Stay hidden! Don't be drawn out by the enemy ahead of God's timing. The fact that Esther is a Jew is hidden from others until the right time. As a matter of fact, her Hebrew name is Hadassah, which means hidden one (Please read my book *Seasons*, chapter 11, for more information on Esther).

In Acts 10:9–23, Peter is on his rooftop praying at

this sixth hour when he sees a vision of unclean animals. God is preparing him to meet three Gentiles who are coming to bring him to Cornelius. The Jews consider the Gentiles to be unclean. Peter goes with them, and God uses him to minister at Cornelius's house, and the whole family is filled with the Holy Ghost (verses 44–48).

As you can see, the sixth hour is also a great time to prepare you to minister to people whom you least expect. Be attentive to God's voice. Get your own pre-conceived ideas out of the way. Cornelius and his family are anxious to hear what Peter has to say. They are hungry for the Word (Acts 10:33). Maybe you are ministering to people who are taking for granted what you are preaching. Maybe God has a group that will gobble up everything you have to say, just like with Peter. Someday at noon, he might start bringing this group to you, searching you out. This group of people may be the least likely you ever expected God to bring your way. Stay open to his prompting.

As I mentioned, this time period is also a great time for God to hide you in his presence from any plans the enemy may have. Stay hidden! Again, don't be drawn out by the enemy ahead of God's timing. Remember in 1 Kings 19:11–12, as Elijah is hiding in the cave, there is a great wind which rends the mountains and breaks rocks. After the wind, there is an earthquake and then a fire. He only comes out when he hears the Lord's small, still voice. Again, stay hidden and wait for God's timing.

In John 4:6, it is recorded that Jesus sits down at the well in Samaria at the sixth hour, or noon. He meets a Samaritan woman there, and there are at least four things that happen at this meeting that affect the future for us:

1. There is a revelation from Jesus about the

living water (verses 10–15). He is talking about receiving the in-filling of the Holy Ghost. This time is an anointed time to receive. God has chosen this time as a special time to indwell his people. Of course, he can in-fill at any time but has chosen this time especially. Come into his presence and receive.

2.   Jesus reveals himself as the Messiah. Pray especially for non-believers to receive this knowledge of who Jesus really is. Most assuredly, Jesus is moving at this time to open hearts. Pray that God removes the blinders and scales from their eyes.

3.   In addition, Jesus moves in the word of knowledge and wisdom so effectively (verses 18, 39–42). He tells not only the lady, but others too, all that is in their hearts. Expect God to pour out through you these and the other gifts, especially at this time.

4.   He also talks about the great harvest that is ready to be harvested (verses 35–36). At this hour, ask him to pour out his gifts to reach the souls that need to be harvested. He tarries there two days (verse 43). He ministers to the people during that time. Look for God to accelerate using you in his gifts at this hour and maybe even continuing the intensity for at least two days.

Here is a summary of possible blessings that can be expected at the noon time hour:

1.   Anointing to receive a blessing from those who wanted to hurt you.

2.   Separation anointing to remove people,

circumstances, and sinful habits from your life once and for all. God can use an unlikely person to remove a problem from your life.

3. Anointing to bring order into families and other everyday situations.

4. Anointing to bless the least likely.

5. Abundance that will never run out.

6. Jesus can reveal more about himself to us in a greater way.

7. Devil is especially bound at this time.

8. God will show up on your behalf.

9. God can start to rain down blessings in your life to let you know that the drought is over.

10. Special time to enter into God's rest.

11. Time to start bringing you out of obscurity.

12. He can also start to make some adjustments to guide us in his way for our lives.

13. Can pour out an anointing on some of us to get at the deepest needs of people.

14. Can anoint some of us to be spiritual carpenters for him to repair people's lives and dreams.

15. To anoint some to give direction and the restoring of paths to some of his children.

17. Blessings of Abraham, Isaac, and Jacob can start to be manifested mightily.

18. God can start bringing judgment on some of your adversaries.

19. God's glory can shine on you in such a greater way that as a result, he could be reversing an enemy attack against you.

20. God can start using you as he promises in Isaiah 61 (i.e." bind up the broken hearted, to proclaim liberty to the captives," etc.).

21. Time to declare war, attack Satan and his works. He is especially weak at this time (12:00 to 3:00 P.M.).

22. Pray for the unsaved at this time; great anointing to call people into his service.

23. Special time to hide from Satan's plans in the presence of your Father.

24. Time to prepare you to minister to people whom you least expect.

25. Special time to receive the in-filling of the Holy Ghost.

26. Special anointing from God to remove blinders from people's hearts so they can really see who Jesus is.

27. An acceleration of God using you in the Gifts of the Spirit.

THIRD HOUR OF THE DAY

(9:00 A.M.)

The third hour of the day is 9:00 A.M. (Again, remember that there is preparation needed before every hourly blessing, especially the hour right before. The devil would like to distract you directly preceding this and every hour of blessing.)

We first hear of this third hour in Matthew 20:3. Here people are called to labor in the vineyard at this hour, according to the parable that Jesus told. On this time of the day, there is such an anointing by God to call people to follow him into service. Be aware of this truth and start praying in that direction around 9:00 A.M. Pray for certain individuals whom God puts on your heart to follow Jesus into his service, to be born again. There is such a wonderful anointing at this time to pray people into the Kingdom. We have to take advantage of God's timing.

In verse 18, Jesus says that he is going to Jerusalem to be betrayed and to die. Accepting this call to the service of Jesus means that you have to follow him no matter where it leads. Paul says in Acts 20:22 that he goes bound in the spirit to Jerusalem, not knowing the things that were waiting there for him. The only thing he knows is that bonds and afflictions are waiting for him there (verse 23). He also says in the next verse that none of these things move him. He was called into God's service and was willing to follow him no matter where he led. He also knew that no weapon formed against him would prosper. He also says in 2 Corinthians 4:18 that he is not influenced by what he sees in the natural. At this hour of the day, God is calling people to follow him, no matter what the cost.

Another revelation about the third hour of the day, or 9:00 A.M., is contained in Acts 2. At this hour (verse 15), the Apostles are in one accord in the temple when suddenly the Spirit of God comes rushing in and fills the house (house of God). (They were in the upper room for prayer but the infilling took place in the temple as the feast of Pentecost was one of the feasts where they were obligated to be in the temple. Please see verse 46 in Acts 2 as the word says "that they continued in the temple"). At this time of the day, God can not only fill you with his Spirit, but also fill every empty area of your life. Believe for God to fill you with his power, if you are not filled, but also to start making all your crooked places straight and your rough places smooth.

People from all over the world who were in Jerusalem came running toward the temple. There is such a strong anointing on this time to attract people to your ministry and to your life in general. Look for God to start increasing his favor in your life at this time. As you pray during this time, believe for this particular moving of God in your life.

Also at this time in the temple, Peter, under the inspiration of the Holy Ghost, says that the "last days" are started, at this hour (verses 16–17). He said that the time Joel prophesied about had started. He mentions in verses 17–21 that certain things would start to happen at this hour (i.e. more people would have dreams and visions from God, that God would pour out more power on his people, that he would show more wonders and signs, etc.). At this hour of the day (9:00 A.M.), we can pray and expect God to manifest himself in these ways in a greater measure!

Also, three thousand people are saved on that day (verse 41). This great harvest starts at this hour. In view of this anointing on this hour, we can pray and believe for a greater harvest of souls (verse 47).

Here is a summary of the possible blessings that can be expected at the third hour of the day, or 9:00 A.M.:

1. Anointing to call people into God's service, and more people will respond, no matter what the cost.

2. Anointing to fill every area of your life!

3. God can begin to attract more people to your ministry.

4. God can begin to show more of his power through signs and wonders in your life.

5. God can pour out more anointing to bring a great harvest of souls.

SEVENTH HOUR OF THE DAY

(1:00 P.M.)

In the Gospel of John 4:46–54, there is a story about the ill son of a nobleman. His father (the nobleman) comes to Jesus and Jesus speaks the word that his son is healed. He believes the word and starts on his way home. On the way home his servants meet him and tell him that the son got better at the seventh hour, or 1:00 P.M. (verse 52). This was the exact time that Jesus said that his son was whole (verse 50).

There is a special healing anointing at this time of day. Of course, God can heal at any time, but he has reserved this time for his healing power to flow. This is a special time, and you need to take advantage of it, especially with a family member who may be sick. Just stand on God's Word and claim the healing anointing that flows from Jesus. He is pouring out at this time, just receive! Just stand on Jesus' Word just like the nobleman does (verse 50). John says in verse 54 that this is the second miracle Jesus performs. Therefore, this seventh hour, or 1:00 P.M., must be important.

Generally, the number seven in the Word means that God is about to complete something, to perfect what is not right. Sickness is something that could render somebody incomplete. At this hour, God can pour out a completion anointing into your life to complete the trial you are going through or to complete a blessing process he has started.

In the Word, the number seven means that the blessing God intends for you to receive by going through a possible trial has already been spoken in heaven and can now be received. It has already been released in the supernatural. It will be revealed in the natural. Hold on! Your victory over the trial has already been assured, if you keep going. Let's look at the Word for the use of the number seven by the Holy Spirit, either in the chapters, or specifically in the passages. In Genesis 7:1, God says that he sees Noah and his family righteous. This means that they will come through their trial with a blessing, no matter what happens to anyone else. God confirms this when he told them to take clean beasts by sevens into the ark. Also, in verse 4, God says it would rain in seven days. This is an additional sign that they will come through their trial, by using the number seven. The mention of rain and the number seven show you also that at this hour, blessings can start to rain on you.

In Genesis 21:29, Abraham gives the enemy king seven lambs in order to enter into a covenant with him. The enemy had been destroying Abraham's wells of water. The king is very upset at what his troops are doing and this covenant ends Abraham's trial.

In Genesis 29:27, the Word says that Jacob would serve another seven years for the hand of Rachel in marriage. The trial of Jacob being tricked by Laban is now over by the use of the number seven.

In Genesis 41, the Word describes the two dreams that the Pharaoh has, and both contain the number seven (verse 1–7). The use of the number seven signifies that the trial that Joseph was going through is now close to being over and the blessing that God intends for him is soon to be realized.

In Exodus 7:4–5, God demonstrates that he already

speaks blessing on his people as they are going through the trial. "Bring my people out of the land of Egypt," and he confirms this by using the number seven in verse 25. The word says in this verse that when God turned the waters into blood, it lasted for seven days.

In Daniel 3:19, King Nebuchadnezzar heats the fiery furnace seven times hotter for the three Hebrew children. This signifies again that God is about to deliver them from their trial and promote them, which happened, as recorded in verse 30.

In Esther 1:10, on the seventh day of the king's feast, Queen Vashti is called to come and perform but refuses. The use of the number seven here signifies that Esther is going to take her place after she goes through preparation and a trial. God is trying to show all who read the book of Esther by the use of the number seven that he will make a way for them through a trial and raise them up to take somebody's place. He will complete the promotion process!

In Psalm 119:164, David says that he would praise God seven times a day because of his righteous judgments. He knew that God would complete judgment in favor for him.

In Acts 6:3, Stephen is chosen to be one of the seven disciples to minister to the widows. The use of the number seven here signifies that Stephen would be persecuted and go through a tremendous trial, but would be promoted. This happens as Stephen is stoned and sees Jesus standing in power. Jesus stands up for him because Stephen didn't deny his name as he is being stoned but asks for the forgiveness of the ones stoning him (Chapter 7:60).

It is so important for you to remember that God has already spoken your portion that you will receive. He has already turned it loose. Just start to receive. He is completing a blessing process that began when the trial you are going through began. Search the Word, and you will see so many scriptures encouraging you at this seventh hour.

NINTH HOUR OF THE DAY

(3:00 P.M.)

This ninth hour of the day is also a time where God calls people into his service as recorded in Matthew 20:5. Believe at this hour for God to stir people up for service, especially loved ones. This is a great time to stand on God's Word and claim this parable in people's lives.

The ninth hour is also when Jesus died. As recorded in Matthew 27:45, there was darkness from the sixth hour (12:00 P.M.) until the ninth hour (3:00 P.M.). Believe that the time when the enemy was moving in your life is over. His attack is over. The power of darkness in the attack is over. You have your victory because of what Jesus accomplished in his death. When Jesus says, "It is finished," the power of Satan is broken. Praise Jesus! He says this at 3:00 P.M. You can do the same by telling the devil that his attack is over. You already have the victory. At this time of the day start proclaiming victory for people whom God puts on your heart. Shout their names and declare victory for them no matter what the situations in their lives look like.

This hour of the day is also an exceptional time of celebration of what Jesus has accomplished for you and me. Take time at this hour to praise him. Take time to worship him. The time allotted to the devil in the trial is over. His time ran out. God controls everything, including the time period of the devil's influence. Isn't God wonderful? At this hour, start enforcing this end of the devil's time by claiming it and praising God for it. God set up this time period for a daily blessing. The devil may have told you that the attack was going to go on forever, but no! It is over at 3:00 P.M. Attack the devil with this promise that his influence is over at this time period because Jesus said so, when he said, "It is finished."

Also at this hour, the veil of the temple is torn by God from top to bottom (Matthew 27:51). Claim at this time, that God is making a way, an opening for you. He is opening a Red Sea for you. He is making a way where there seems to be no way. No matter who or what is against you, claim this breakthrough at this time. Claim that just as the veil of the temple is torn by God, he has made a way for you. Of course, we know God can make a way at any time, but there is a special anointing at this time of day. Also claim breakthroughs for others, for God to make a way for them also. Lift up their names before him.

Also at this hour, graves open and many bodies of the saints arise (verse 52). There is a special anointing at this hour for God to break people out of their situations. Where they may feel buried under the circumstances, God's resurrection power is now there to bring them out! God rubs this right in Satan's face. Satan thought he had you buried under worry, sickness, fear, doubt, and uncertainty, but here comes God at 3:00 P.M. to bust you out. He makes a way out after Satan did all that he could do to prevent your breakout of his prison. It doesn't matter how long Satan has had you buried or how deep. When this hour rolls around, claim your deliverance based on what happened at 3:00 P.M. on the day Jesus gave up his life. We don't have to wait for Resurrection Sunday to receive resurrection power. This is a daily time to receive this power over the circumstances coming against you!

Allow the same power that busted Jesus out of the tomb, and these others at the time he died, bust you out of the mess you are in. Be untied and untie others.

This special time of 3:00 P.M., when Jesus died and bodies of some saints arose, could also be pointing to the Rapture. The Word says in 1 Thessalonians 4:14, "for if we believe that Jesus died and rose again, even so them also which sleep in Jesus will God bring with him."

In verse 16, the Word says that the *dead in Christ will rise first*. From my book *Seasons,* we know that the Rapture of the Church will take place on some Feast of Trumpets (Rosh HaShannah) in the future. Could this event also happen at 3:00 P.M. (Jerusalem time, since we all go up together)? This is the greatest blessing that could ever happen at 3:00 P.M. Also, the Word talks about the Rapture occurring at the *Last Trump* (1 Corinthians 15:52). The armies of Israel would assemble in a pre-arranged location at the sound of the first trump then begin to march at the sound of the second trump. The Word also says in Revelation 8:1 that there was silence in heaven for a half hour. Is it possible that we will be waiting to hear the second trump and this could explain the silence for a half an hour? Could the first trump be for us to assemble together in the spirit at 2:30 P.M. or a half hour before the Rapture at 3:00 P.M.? I am not predicting, but these possibilities are really amazing!

Here is a summary of the possible blessings that can be expected at the ninth hour of the day or 3:00 P.M.:

1. Call people into service.

2. Defeat for the enemy. Claim it for those under attack.

3. God will start making a way of break-through for you.

4. God pours out his resurrection power.

ELEVENTH HOUR OF THE DAY

(5:00 P.M.)

In Matthew 20:9, people who are hired at the last hour (eleventh) get as much as the others who start working earlier. This is truly the time of day when the Lord raises up those who are considered last and makes them the first. Be aware of this time. You may feel that God has forgotten about you, but no!

This is the time of day when God starts replacing Saul's with David's (people after his own heart). He is replacing Moses' with Joshua's, Eli's with Samuel's. This is the time where God is raising up nobodys. This is the time when God will bring some who are considered the least to become the greatest! God has a perfect timing for everyone who is part of his plan.

Remember in Genesis 26, Isaac is digging up the wells of water that his father, Abraham, had dug originally, but the Philistines keep stopping them up. However, in verse 22, Isaac digs a well that the enemy couldn't tamper with. The name they give to the well was Rehoboth (the Lord hath made room for us). Right after that, the enemy comes to Isaac and wants to sign a covenant with him. God is pushing your enemies back and making room for you. It is his timing for you to take someone's place. He is making the last to be the first.

At the time that God anointed David, an evil spirit came on Saul, the king. God had started the process of David taking his place. Some people get lifted up in the flesh and feel that the whole body of Christ revolves around them. They are sadly mistaken. God could be ready to replace them. He may have already started the process. He always has a ram in the bush. He is starting to remove the candlestick (authority and purpose) from people's lives.

When God raises one up, that person has to realize that only the anointing of God can do it. He has to realize that the only way he can do the assignment is by that same anointing. When we read chapter 17, we can see how David avails himself of this anointing. It looks like an impossible situation with both armies lining up against each other and Goliath leading the way for the enemy. Every Israelite is afraid of him, including Saul, who is the biggest Israelite. God makes the right choice in replacing Saul with David.

Those whom God calls, he also justifies. In verses 4–7, God shows how big Goliath is to let us know that we need to factor in and rely on the anointing of God. The anointing of God on us can do what we can never do. In verse 23, the Word records that David hears the great words Goliath is speaking against David's God, and this gets David angry. Saul tries to talk David out of going against Goliath but to no avail. David knew that the anointing of God is greater than anything that could come against him and has a practiced faith in the anointing of God. He points out to Saul that when a lion and bear attacked his sheep, the anointing of God came upon him and he slew them with his own hands. He knew this same anointing would defeat any adversary.

Whatever God is asking you to do, factor in the anointing. He wants to raise you up out of nowhere, but you have to rely on the anointing and not on your own intelligence and strength. He wants to raise you up and show others what he can do with a fully surrendered life. He gets all the glory.

In 1 Samuel 17:37, David tells Saul that the same God who destroyed the lion and the bear will defeat the giant. David knew the attack is not against the Israelites but against God. He separates himself from the attack and turns the battle over to God. If you are working for Jesus and people are attacking you, you have to realize it is a spiritual battle and the forces of evil are trying to align against God. They can't defeat God. They want to fight *you*. Goliath is looking for a *man* to fight him (1 Samuel 17:10).

God uses David to do some great things. This is somebody who had been tending sheep just a little while before. God raises him up out of nowhere and uses him mightily.

He wants to do the same with you. Just decrease in the flesh, so his anointing can be increased out of you. Follow God's direction and correction for your faults. Turn every problem you have in the flesh over to him. "Through the Spirit you can mortify the deeds of the flesh" (Romans 8:13). Make your number one prayer to be conformed to the image of Jesus and watch how he increases the anointing in your life to have you win battles for him that nobody else can win. He truly wants to make somebodys out of nobodys.

You may feel that you are last on his list for promotion, but he wants to turn the list upside down and make you the first! He can start doing this at the eleventh hour.

MIDNIGHT

In Exodus 12:29, the Word mentions that God kills all the firstborn in the land of Egypt in order to persuade them to let his people go. This midnight hour is a time of deliverance, especially for God's people. Just like God's people had to be ready to go, so should we be ready to move when he wants.

In verse 35, the Egyptians give them gold and silver. This midnight hour is a great time to start believing for the wealth of your enemies to start coming to you. Believe for God's favor to be turned loose on you.

This midnight hour of deliverance (sixth hour of the night) is also contained in Judges 16:2–3. The Philistines have Samson locked behind the gates of the city, but Samson breaks out and picks up the gates and carries them all the way up Mount Hebron at midnight. The Philistines can't hold Samson, and your enemies can't control or keep you bound. Receive your release from whatever or whoever is trying to control you at this midnight hour.

Another truth about the midnight hour is contained in Ruth 3:8. Ruth lies at the feet of Boaz at midnight. He chooses her to be his wife, and the next day, claims her before the whole city as his kinsman. For us, this means lying at the feet of our kinsman redeemer, Jesus. We can be blessed at any time of the day, but this is a special time when our Redeemer wants to let us know we are special to him.

Another aspect of the midnight hour is contained in Psalm 119:62. The psalmist says that at midnight he will "rise to give thanks unto God for his righteous judgments." This is a great time for God to start judging on your behalf. Believe that whoever is trying to come against you unjustly will be judged by God. He will rule on your behalf and settle the issue. It doesn't matter if a whole company is coming against you. If you are doing the righteous thing he will defend and vindicate you. Praise him!

In Matthew 25, there is a familiar parable about the ten virgins. Five are ready and five aren't. At midnight, the bridegroom comes. Look for the bridegroom (Jesus) to come on the scene at this time to give you a new beginning. Look for promotion to start. Just be ready. Watch and expect him to come on the scene of your difficulties and bring about your new beginning. Please make sure that your number one prayer is to conform to the image of Jesus and watch how he starts to promote at this hour.

In Luke 11, there is another great truth about this hour. Jesus tells a parable about a man knocking on a friend's door at midnight, looking for bread. He said in verse 9, "Ask and it shall be given you; seek and ye shall find; knock and it shall be opened unto you." God is telling us to knock on the door of his heart at this time to receive, and keep knocking or believing, until he grants your request. He is in such a time of giving at this midnight hour!

The truth about God's deliverance anointing at this hour is also confirmed in Acts chapter 16; Paul and Silas are thrown into the deepest, most inner part of the prison. There seems to be no hope, but an earthquake comes and God sets them free (verse 26) at midnight.

Paul also goes to the jailer's house (at midnight), and the whole family gets saved (verses 31–34). Take advantage of this time.

The anointing on this hour for salvation is also contained in Acts 20:8–11. While Paul is preaching (midnight), a little boy falls and dies. God raises this boy from the dead through Paul. God wants to raise up the spiritually dead at this time and save their souls. The Word says in Ephesians 2:1 that he quickened us who were dead in trespasses and sins. He wants to quicken others at this time.

Another truth about this time is contained in Acts 27:27; Paul and the others in the ship in the midst of the storm are encouraged when they learn that they are getting closer to land (at midnight), closer to their deliverance. At this midnight hour God wants to speak to your spirit and confirm how close you are to breakthrough. Praise him!

Here is a summary of the possible blessings that can be expected at the midnight hour:

1. Deliverance.

2. God can show favor in your life by judging on your behalf.

3. Look for the bridegroom (Jesus) to come on the scene to give you a new beginning.

4. Start knocking on the door of his heart in earnest and it will be given. Keep knocking. He is always a God of giving, especially at this hour.

5. Salvation. Expect God to move whole families to be saved. Just believe!

6. God wants to confirm to you how close you are to breakthrough.

Be in his presence at this time and see how he reveals these promises in your life at the midnight hour.

FIRST, SECOND, THIRD, AND FOURTH WATCH OF THE NIGHT

In Acts 23, the Word talks about a plot by about forty men to kill the Apostle Paul. Paul's nephew overhears them and warns Claudius Lysias, the chief captain, who has Paul in prison (verses 12–35). Claudius sends Paul to Felix for safety with a guard of two hundred soldiers, seventy horsemen and two hundred spearmen. This happens at the third hour of the night, or 9:00 P.M. or during the first watch of the night. The first watch of the night is from 6:00 P.M. to 9:00 P.M. As a result of this incident, God is letting us know that there is a great anointing at this time to deliver his people from a serious plot of the enemy and to use somebody to help prevent Satan's success. Look for God to provide a way of escape from a situation you may be in at this time and please take advantage of the person or persons God uses to help you.

In Luke 12:36, Jesus talks about servants watching for their lord or master to come. He says that the people who watch for their master's coming sit down to eat with him and he will serve them (verse 37). Jesus says in verse 38 that if the master comes in the second or third watch and finds them alert and looking for his coming, then they are blessed.

This is a great promise to you and me. The second watch of the night is from 9:00 P.M. to midnight. The third watch of the night is midnight to 3:00 A.M. At these times especially, we need to expect Jesus, our Lord and Master, to communicate to us in a special way (sit down to eat) and minister to our greatest need (serve us).

He is not a God who is way out in the universe someplace, but rather, he is inside of us and moving on our situation with his power. At these times, expect him to move for you. If you are lying in bed at these times, meditate on who he is and how he sanctified these watches to communicate with us in a special way and minister to our greatest needs. Expect to feel the closeness of God especially in these time periods. He may wake you up just to love on you or give you special revelations. He may communicate to you through dreams. He may wake you up to intercede for someone, or even for whole nations. These are great revelationary and intercessory times.

The fourth watch of the night occurs between 3:00 A.M. and 6:00 A.M. In Matthew 14:24, there is an account of the apostles in a ship tossing to and fro by a storm. In the fourth watch of the night, Jesus walks on the sea (verse 25). As soon as he got into the ship, the wind ceases and they make it to the other side. This is a special time for Jesus to come during the darkest hour of your trial and walk on the very thing that is so big against you. Take solace in the fact that everything and everyone was created by Jesus and for Jesus. This includes Satan and all thrones, principalities, powers, and dominions (Colossians 1:16–18). Jesus is truly on top of your situation. During this time he wants to demonstrate this fact and show his awesome power in your situation.

At these times, he also wants to take you to the other side. He wants to show you how close you are to your destiny and how he is pouring out his power to make room for you in his kingdom plan. Turn over every concern and obstacle that you have to him and let him make a way for you. It doesn't matter who or what is coming against you to try to thwart your destiny. Whether it is a person or an organization that is trying to hinder or stop you, they have to get out of the Lord's way or be forced out of his way. Also, the Lord uses these intimate evening watches to prepare us for the daily hourly blessings, as well as to intercede for others. In addition, He wants to bring instruction, encouragement, and possibly correction to us during these watches.

MONTHLY BLESSINGS

Besides God's hourly blessings which we have just discussed, blessings are contained in certain significant days in particular months of the year as well as certain months as a whole. Please remember that God can bless at any time, but he has anointed and set aside certain months to perform special and unique blessings. In the next succeeding chapters we will study each month and learn the blessings associated with the months as a whole and the particular days within these months. At the end of the book I have included charts to show the correlation between the days on the Gregorian calendar, as they correspond to the blessing times according to the word, by using the Hebrew calendar. As you look at the Hebrew calendar just remember that the day (according to the Word) starts at evening the previous day, and ends on evening the same day. Also, when talking of a blessing from the word that occurs in the seventh month, for example, I am not talking about the month of July on the Gregorian calendar but the month Tishrei which occurs between September and October. The secret to know when an exact blessing period occurs, please refer from the Hebrew calendar back to our calendar or the Gregorian calendar.

The months of the year are as follows:

First Month	Nisan	Mar-Apr.
Second Month	Iyar	Apr-May
Third Month	Sivan	May-June

Fourth Month	Tammuz	June-July
Fifth Month	Av	July-Aug.
Sixth Month	Elul	Aug-Sept.
Seventh Month	Tishrei	Sept.-Oct.
Eighth Month	Cheshvan	Oct.-Nov.
Ninth Month	Kislev	Nov.-Dec.
Tenth Month	Tevet	Dec.- Jan.
Eleventh Month	Shevat	Jan.- Feb.
Twelfth Month	Adar	Feb.-Mar.

EXAMPLE from www.hebcal.com/hebcal

March 2010

Sunday	Monday	Tuesday	Wednesday	Thursday	Friday	Saturday
	1 — 15th of Adar, 5770	2 — 16th of Adar, 5770	3 — 17th of Adar, 5770	4 — 18th of Adar, 5770	5 — 19th of Adar, 5770	6 — 20th of Adar, 5770
7 — 21st of Adar, 5770	8 — 22nd of Adar, 5770	9 — 23rd of Adar, 5770	10 — 24th of Adar, 5770	11 — 25th of Adar, 5770	12 — 26th of Adar, 5770	13 — 27th of Adar, 5770
14 — 28th of Adar, 5770	15 — 29th of Adar, 5770	16 — 1st of Nisan, 5770	17 — 2nd of Nisan, 5770	18 — 3rd of Nisan, 5770	19 — 4th of Nisan, 5770	20 — 5th of Nisan, 5770
21 — 6th of Nisan, 5770	22 — 7th of Nisan, 5770	23 — 8th of Nisan, 5770	24 — 9th of Nisan, 5770	25 — 10th of Nisan, 5770	26 — 11th of Nisan, 5770	27 — 12th of Nisan, 5770
28 — 13th of Nisan, 5770	29 — 14th of Nisan, 5770	30 — 15th of Nisan, 5770	31 — 16th of Nisan, 5770			

FIRST MONTH

Nisan (Mar.-Apr.)

In Joel 2:23, God mentions through the prophet Joel that he wants to pour out the former and latter rain in the first month. The first month of the year starts on Nisan, which is our equivalent of March-April.

God said in this verse that up to that point he had poured out the rain moderately, but it is about to change. Are you ready for change? He is ready to get extravagant with his blessings. He says in verse 24 that "the floors shall be full of wheat and the vats shall overflow with wine and oil." He is ready, if you are, for you to be on the receiving end of his extravagant blessings. For some of you, it has been such a drought. There is an overflow anointing on this first month. Receive it!

Allow God to mortify the deeds of your flesh daily and make your number one prayer that God would conform you to the image of Jesus. When you have done this, you are in position to receive this overflow blessing anointing in this month. Praise him!

He also says in verse 25 that he would restore years into your life (i.e. take away the effect of events that happened years ago). He can restore in such a marvelous way that the event may seem to have not happened at all. He can also start in this month to restore monies and other assets that were taken from you.

He also says in verse 26 that you will not be ashamed. You have believed for a long time for God to bring some blessings into your life that he has promised you. He is saying that you will not be ashamed. During this month, he can start to bring some of these promises to pass. Just believe. God also says that he would "pour out his Spirit on all flesh" in verse 28. Believe that he will start pouring out his Spirit on family members and others you are concerned about.

In Numbers 20:1–11, Moses writes how the children of Israel murmurs and complains when they had no water and Moses is being tested and hits the rock, instead of speaking to the rock, as he was commanded by God. This happened during the first month (verse 1). This first month can also be a time of testing and you need to be on guard. As a result of this, Moses is not allowed to enter into the Promised Land (verse 23–24). All he could do was see it from a distance. Please don't give up on God merely because circumstances are not lining up as quickly as you would like. Don't murmur and complain. You don't want to lose blessings, do you? Just as the first month of the year can be a time of great blessing, it can also be a time of great testing before the blessing is manifested.

Just like Moses was separated from going into the Promise Land, this first month is also a time where God will separate people from their purposes or destinies and give them to someone else. Look at David taking Saul's place, Joshua taking Moses' place and Samuel taking Eli's place.

In Numbers 21:1–35, the Canaanites attack Israel. The first month is also a time of war. In verse 35, Moses records that Israel possesses the land of the enemy. This is a time for you get spoils from the sinners ("The wealth of the sinner is laid up for the just." [Proverbs 13:22]). Your enemies may initiate the attack, but God is allowing the attack in order to give you their possessions. It is all in God's plans. If you see the enemy attack in this month, you have to realize that the attack was all set up by God to bless you, not to harm you.

In Isaiah 35, God is preparing his people for an attack of the enemy by saying in verses 1 and 2 that they will blossom abundantly and rejoice. Sure enough, the enemy attacks, and they are defeated by God (37:36). As you can see, this month is a time of you getting spoils from the enemy, no matter what it looks like when you are initially attacked. Remember, spoils are something people don't want you to have, but God says he will give it to you anyway. Remember, especially in this first month, that "everything and everybody was created by God and for him" (Colossians 1:16). He is the boss.

The Israelites crossed the Jordan River in the first month (1 Chronicles 12:15). The first month is a time for many to cross over into purpose, no matter how deep your Jordan River seems. God will make a way where there seems to be no way, when your back may be up against a wall.

The first month is also a time for a change in leadership. In 2 Chronicles 35:21, Josiah, a king of Israel, is told by God not to go against the king of Egypt. He did not listen and is killed in battle (verses 22–24). There is a replacement anointing on this month, especially around Passover because this is the time this event happens (verses 1–19). "Promotion comes from God; he puts down one and sets up another" (Psalm 75:6–7). He may be preparing you to take someone's place.

In Ezra 7:9, the Word says that Ezra begins to travel to Jerusalem to rebuild the temple on the first day of the first month. On this particular day of the month, God could put an assignment on you that could change many people's lives and bring glory to God. Please be ready and attentive to hear the voice of the Lord, especially at this time. The favor of God on Ezra was so strong that Artaxerxes, the king of Persia, gives Ezra a letter directing people to take care of his every need as he does his assignment (verse 11). Do you realize that the same favor of God is on you at this time? So step out in faith, with God's backing.

In Ezekiel 29:17–19, in the first month, God mentions that Nebuchadnezzar, king of Babylon, did not receive wages in his battle against Tyrus. God didn't forget about this and promises him the land of Egypt as a spoil for him and to supply the lost wages for his army. God is such a kind and merciful God! He will never forget your labor for his name. Just get ready to begin to receive at this time. What you might have considered lost in the past is not lost to God. He is truly a God of restitution and recovery (Acts 3:21), especially at this first day of the first month.

On the seventh day of the first month God broke the power of Pharaoh, king of Egypt, as recorded in Ezekiel 30:20–24. He strengthens the power of the king of Babylon against him and puts his sword into his hand. God says that "vengeance is his" (Hebrews 10:30). So this is also a great day for God to take away the power of your enemies, strengthen you, and put the sword of the Word into your hands, in order to complete the victory. It doesn't matter to God how long your enemies seem to have been winning. On this day, expect God to move on your behalf and break their power. God will divide their tongues and bring confusion into their midst. They will turn on each other (2 Chronicles 20:23). God will get all the glory!

In Ezra 8:31, Ezra and others take the gold and silver

meant for the temple of God through some enemy territory. God's protection is great upon them. This occurs on the twelfth day of the first month. Expect God to start to bring the finances for your ministry on this day, no matter how much the enemy doesn't want them to arrive. God will make sure you get what you need as you do his will.

The Feast of Passover occurs on the fourteenth day of Nisan, which is the first month. It is fourteen days after the first of the year. Passover is an appointed time to remember Jesus' death and to remember that his sacrificial death purchased our deliverance from sin and Satan. Jesus rose from the dead three days later on Nisan 17. This is a time to take advantage of God's anointing on this time of the month and die to our fleshly desires and weaknesses.

We can also give situations that are troubling us to him and let him rectify them and bring us out as victors. If we obey him during this season and submit these troubled areas to him, there is no telling what joyful blessings he can now bring into our lives. Just as he rose three days later on Nisan 17, we can have that same resurrection power raise us up into victory over those troubled areas of our lives. One reason there are so many hurting and burdened Christians is that they don't recognize this season of deliverance and resurrection. They miss this anointed season from God to accomplish their much-needed freedom.

This is truly a wonderful time of the month and many mighty miracles could be unleashed by God. It is all about his timing. We just need to recognize how he wants to move. Discover the end result he is attempting to accomplish in your life during this particular time of the month.

God also wants to use this time to bring us to new levels by that same power that raised Jesus from the dead. Praise him! The Jews were delivered from the Egyptians at the Red Sea on Nisan 17, the same day Jesus rose. Esther and the other Jews were also delivered from Haman on Nisan 17. Noah's Ark rested on Mount Ararat on the same day. This is surely a great time of deliverance, restoration, and resurrection to new levels. I pray that you take advantage of these anointed days during the first month.

The next Feast Day during this month is the Feast of Unleavened Bread, which is a seven-day Feast that starts the day after Passover. It starts on Nisan 15 and ends on Nisan 21. The Jews are told to remove all leaven from their houses during this time period (Lev. 23:6). Leaven is a type of sin. This season is a period of time where God wants to purify us. Jesus fulfilled this feast by leading a sinless life.

As a reminder, during this monthly time and in every month, God wants access to change us into the image of Jesus. There is such a special anointing during this time that the things and people that you allow him to remove out of your life may never come back.

Most Christians don't realize the power in God's monthly blessings and carry their sins and circumstances from one season to another. It is similar to putting the garbage out to be picked up. There are certain days that garbage is picked up. It would be foolish to put the garbage out on days that there is no pickup. But when it is the right time, all the garbage you leave out will be picked up. The people picking up the trash will not bring it back. All the garbage you allow God to pick up during this time will be removed once and for all. Only you can allow garbage back into your life. This is such a powerful blessing during this month. Take advantage of it.

Another thing God wants to remove from our lives, especially during this time of the first month, is the Goliath who is dictating your life. David knows he could destroy all the Philistines if he killed Goliath (1 Samuel 17), since the giant was their leader. Goliath was the one doing all the threatening. The other Philistines were hiding behind him.

In Numbers 33:3, the Word mentions that the children of Israel leave Egypt on the fifteenth day of the first month. They also leave with a high hand. They get gold and silver from the Egyptians. Even though God can deliver at any time, this is a day of great deliverance. Begin to move out of where you are as God's deliverance power moves in your life. The Israelites were in bondage for many years, but this day God moved on their behalf and they had to move by faith. When Peter was in prison, as recorded in Acts 12, he rises up and moves when the angel tells him to (verse 7).

On the sixteenth day of the first month the feast of firstfruits occurs. It is a fifty-day feast that ends on the sixth day of Sivan, or Pentecost. As Pentecost approaches, God has chosen this time to do some spring cleaning. This starts to happen during the time of firstfruits. After Jesus rose from the dead, he ascended to his Father to present his blood on the mercy seat of heaven to cleanse it. He did this during firstfruits, to show that he is the Firstfruit from the dead.

On this feast previously, the High Priest would present the first grain from the harvest to God as an offering. Jesus fulfilled this feast after he rose from the dead. During this time, God is trying to prepare us for his mighty move that will start to take place on Pentecost.

Allow him to point out those areas of your life that need to change. He is trying to get his people ready for all that he is starting on Pentecost.

During this time, your number one prayer should be for the Father to conform you into the image of Jesus. As you pray this from the heart, he will point out those areas of your life that need to change. Just because we are saved, it doesn't mean that we have arrived. God put us on the road to sanctification, when we became born again, but holiness is a process that must be walked out. Even though we receive a righteous standing when born again, the road to sanctification is a process that conforms us to the image of Jesus. During our walk on this road, God wants complete access to change us into his image. As God points things out in our life, we can't argue with him and deny, but need to accept the correction and allow him to change us. The Word says in Romans 8:13, that only the Spirit of God can mortify the deeds of the flesh!

We are helpless to change ourselves and stop sinning. However, we need to make quality decisions not to sin and ask for his strength. How many blessings God can bestow on us with this attitude! This is why we have missed blessings. God was trying to prepare us for blessings during his cleaning process, but we went back to our old ways and missed him.

In Romans, Paul says "we should not serve sin," that we are dead to sin (6:6, 11). He also says in v. 12 not to let sin reign in our mortal bodies, that we should obey it in the lust thereof. He also says in verse 13 "not to yield our members (bodies) as instruments of unrighteousness unto sin, but yield our members as instruments of righteousness unto God." Sin has no power over us unless we yield to it. Satan can't make us sin; he only tempts our flesh. This is why we need to know that the battle is over our thought life.

In 2 Corinthians 10:5, Paul instructs us to cast down all evil imaginations and bring every thought captive to Jesus. This process is like a tennis game. When the devil gives you a thought, hit it back to Jesus. Please don't dwell and meditate on the thought. Most murderers don't become killers overnight. They meditate on the thought that the enemy gives over a period of time, act it out in their minds, and then perform the terrible act. The Word even tells us what to think on in Philippians 4:8: things that are true, honest, just, pure, lovely, good report, virtue, and praise. We have to realize that there is a battle over our minds to try to control our future destiny away from the purpose God intends.

We have a responsibility in our walk to make a quality decision not to sin, to repent quickly if we commit a sin, and to walk circumspectively, avoiding pitfalls and plans of the enemy. Paul says in 1 Corinthians 9:26, 27 to bring our bodies under subjection, lest we become castaways. Temptation is strong, but Paul also says in 10:13 that God always prepares a way of escape. Praise him!

During this spring cleaning, God wants us to clean ourselves with his Word. He wants us to speak these scriptures into our lives. Before you confess scriptures over yourself, say out loud that "the scriptures that I am claiming are for me and my family and I am using the terms *we* or *us* to apply these scriptures to my family and me." In reality, you are cleaning your whole family with the Word. For example, in Romans 6:14, you can say that sin does not have dominion over us. The devil knows exactly whom you are taking about because you said in the very beginning whom the scriptures apply to.

This is a powerful weapon that can clean you up on a daily basis.

Please take note of this spring cleaning process and allow God to change you into the image of his Son. He wants to do this cleaning not only at this time of year, but anytime that he prompts you! When he has access to change you, there is no telling what he can do to bless you, especially during a season such as Pentecost. As you see all the blessings, contained in this feast, you will be glad that you went through the Spring Cleaning.

On the seventeenth day of the first month is when Jesus rose from the dead. That same resurrection power that raised him from the dead is available to you to raise you up out of any situation that has you buried. The greatest event in history occurred in this first month on this day. Surely his resurrection power is available at other times, but it is always available on this day. Believe when that day comes around for that same resurrection power to raise you up from any situation.

Also, on the seventeenth day of the first month, or Nisan 17, the Jews, as recorded in the book of Esther, were delivered from wicked Haman on Nisan 17. In Esther 3:12, the decree to kill all the Jews is signed on the thirteenth day of the first month, or Nisan 13. On the same day as recorded in chapter 4, Mordecai approaches Esther about the plan that wicked Haman tricked the King into signing. She tells him to tell the people to fast for her for three days and that she would go in to see the King unannounced (on Nisan 16). The King receives her and wants to give her anything that she wants (Oh! the favor of God!). She asks (verse 4) that Haman would be invited to a banquet she was giving on that day (Nisan 16). At the banquet she asks the king that Haman be invited to another banquet that she would give the next day (Nisan 17). On this day, at this banquet, it was revealed to the King that Haman was behind the plan to kill all of Esther's people. The King hanged Haman on the same gallows that Haman prepared for Mordecai on that very day (Nisan 17). So Nisan 17 is a great day for God to demonstrate his deliverance power in your life.

In Daniel 10:4, the angel Gabriel appears to Daniel and shows him things that were going to happen in the last days. This happened on the twenty-fourth day of the first month. This is a great day of visitation by God to speak a prophetic word that could affect the whole world. In verse 2, Daniel mentions that he started to fast for twenty-one days. In verse 13, Gabriel mentions that the Prince of Persia withstood him twenty-one days. It would seem that Daniel started his fast on the third day of the first month. This fast helps to bring an angelic visitation twenty-one days later, when Gabriel appears. As a result, the third day of the first month is a great day to start a Daniel fast (verse 3) that could bring about an angelic visitation or a far reaching word from the Lord, concerning the last days.

Let's summarize the importance of the first month as a whole:

1. Extravagant blessings.
2. Restoration.
3. Fulfillment of long-awaited promises.
4. New strategies.
5. Time of testing, be on guard.
6. Transfer of assignments to others.
7. Time of war and to receive spoils.
8. Cross-over into purpose.

9. Change in leadership, replacement anointing.

10. God raises up promises that seem to be dead, and he can bring one to new spiritual levels.

11. God takes away the power of your enemies, destroys their plans, brings judgment on them, and brings a great deliverance.

A summary of the importance of specific days in the month:

1. First day- assignments given to change many lives, time to step out, and there is also a recovery and restoration anointing on this day.

2. Seventh day- God taking away the power of your enemies.

3. Fourteenth day- Feast of Passover- A special time to die to your fleshly desires and weaknesses. Destroy those circumstances in your life that are interfering with receiving God's blessings. Passover anointing to deliver whole families.

4. Fifteenth day to the twenty-first day- Feast of the Unleavened Bread. Unleavened Bread anointing to remove things from your life that are contrary to God's Word (your Goliaths and other strongholds, etc) once and for all.

5. Fifteenth day- Great deliverance anointing and an anointing to receive spoils from enemies.

6. Sixteenth day- Feast of Firstfruits - Feast of Firstfruits anointing to do a "spring cleaning" in our lives, to enable us by the power of the Holy Spirit to conform to the image of Jesus.

7. Seventeenth day- Christ's resurrection - God can raise up promises that seem to be dead and he can bring one to new spiritual levels, all with his Resurrection power.

8. Seventeenth day- God can bring great deliverance from the plans of your enemies and bring them into judgment.

9. Twenty-fourth- great day of visitation and revelation, especially new truths of the Last Days.

During this month, you may feel all alone with nobody who can help you but God. This is the way he wants you to feel. He is preparing you for something powerful during the year. The weird feeling of being alone is necessary for God to bring you to a new level of promotion and blessing. The number one, as used in the Word, means that you are the one going through the trial. Other people may be affected indirectly, but you are the one whom God has called to go through a particular trial in order to receive the blessing he has for you. During this first month, don't look for a lot of help from people because God is trying to establish a closer relationship with you.

The numbering of chapters and verses in the Word bear witness to the truth that God has shown me about his numbering system. For example, in Mark 1, the Word tells of John being the voice crying in the wilderness and the one whom God uses to preach the baptism in the wilderness. God is showing in Mark 1 that he calls us alone and uses us as individuals. In this same chapter, the Word shows how Jesus is used by his Father to call people to follow him, to cast out devils, etc. I think it is amazing that the Bible talks about how God deals with us as one, uses us as one, and shows what he can do with one person.

In Luke 1, the Word follows the calling of Zacharias and his doubt and eventual belief. It also talks of Elizabeth conceiving and encouraging Mary, the mother of Jesus. It tells of Mary, the one person chosen by God to carry his Son, after the Holy Spirit overshadows her (verse 35). The chapter shows how God calls people alone to go through a trial or on an assignment and the eventual blessing.

In John 1, the Word talks again about one called John the Baptist being called, being used by God and finding Jesus the Messiah. It talks about Jesus calling individuals—Nathaniel and Phillip. Do you see the numbering of Chapter 1 with the calling of us as one, called for our individual trials, called for our individual ministries and blessings? Praise him!

In Jeremiah 1, the Word talks of Jeremiah being called before the foundation of the world (verse 5). In verse 8, the Word shows that he believes that he was not worthy and how God encourages him. In verse 10, God tells him his purpose: "to root out, to pull down, to destroy, to build..." Again, it's the calling of one person for his work. This should encourage us to know that God calls and treats us as individuals.

In Proverbs 1, God introduces Solomon—one man—to write proverbs in order to know wisdom and instruction. He is writing to his son and to us. Again, one man called for a purpose. Be encouraged that God has called you as one man, woman, boy, or girl for his purpose and anoints you to do so and to go through whatever trial is necessary to get your blessing.

In Revelation 1, God introduces John, his servant, and how he sends and signifies the Revelation of Jesus Christ. This is the beginning of a great revelation to John for us. What a blessing. What an honor for John. It's the only book in the Word where Jesus is called "The Alpha and the Omega, the Beginning and the End" (verse 8). Look how God used one person to reveal so much and how God wants to use you as an individual and give great revelations to you also.

Another example is in Acts 1:26; Matthias is called by God to replace Judas. This is an individual calling of one person.

In Genesis 1 verse 26, he relates how he creates an individual (Adam) in his image for a purpose. This is important for us to know, that Satan can't touch us successfully on a mission from God because we have been individually hand-picked by God.

In summary, be encouraged during this first month, that you are not alone. God is with you. He is preparing you during this first month in a very personal way for him to use you so powerfully during the rest of the year. During this month, God is really trying to show you that all you need is him.

Here are some important additional facts about the first month: It is my belief after studying the word that Jesus was born on Passover, which as I mentioned, occurs in the first month. In the book of Luke 2:41 the word says that Jesus' parents went to Jerusalem every year at Passover. In v. 42, the word says (in the Greek) that when Jesus became twelve years old they went to Jerusalem after the custom of the feast. (Passover was followed by

Unleavened Bread, which was a seven-day feast in which the first and last days were holy convocations where they were obligated to be in the temple-Lev. 23:6-8). The word also says in Luke that Mary and Joseph could not find Jesus and went a day's journey back to their relatives to try to find him (Luke 2:43, 44). So, you can see that he became twelve on Passover and they traveled one day to be in the temple on the first day of the Feast of Unleavened Bread.

Also, a male child was circumcised on the eighth day after his birth (Lev. 12:3). When Jesus was born on Passover he was circumcised on the eighth day (Passover plus seven days of Unleavened Bread), which was the last day of Unleavened Bread. So, Jesus fulfilled Passover by being born and dying on Passover. He fulfilled Unleavened Bread by leading a sinless life and being circumcised on the last day of Unleavened Bread. As I mentioned earlier Jesus rose from the dead on Nisan 17, also fulfilling Unleavened Bread which occurs during Nisan 15-21.

Some try to say that Jesus was born on the first day of the Feast of Tabernacles, based on Zacharias, the father of John the Baptist. They try to figure the date of the birth of Jesus from the course in the temple that Zacharias had to serve (Luke 1:5-10). However, they don't realize that he served two courses, one six months later in the year. Also, they had to serve on three holidays; Passover, Pentecost, and Tabernacles. So, it is difficult to know when Zacharias was serving in the Temple and as a result when John the Baptist was conceived.

The events of the first month show God's precise timing. Let the same spirit that raised Jesus from the dead quicken you to a new level during this first month.

SECOND MONTH

Iyyar (Apr.-May)

We now want to explore the great truths in the Word concerning the second month; In Numbers 1:1–3, God speaks to Moses to gather all the men who could go to war. This is an excellent time to take an inventory of the people in your ministry to see if they have strength for spiritual war. This is a time where God will speak to you about the strengths and weaknesses of the people around you. He'll let you know whom you can trust to line up behind you in battle against Satan. It is so important to listen to the Holy Spirit about whom you can trust, especially during this month. In any battle fought in the World Wars, it was critical who fought next to you. You were only as strong as your "buddy" next to you. It is obvious that David recognized this great fact by the men he assembled around him, as recorded in 2 Sam. 23:8–39. Some even risk their lives to get him a drink of water in Jerusalem (verse 16).

Also during this month, as recorded in Numbers 2, God tells Moses to position the people by families around the tabernacle. It is also so important, especially at this time, to position more prayer covering around you and your ministry. Try to get volunteers to take a certain time during the day to pray, and try to organize a twenty-four-hour prayer clock around you and your ministry. You may be only as strong as the prayer around you.

In Numbers 10:11, the Word says the cloud is taken up off the tabernacle and the children of Israel have to move to another location. This happens on the twentieth day of the second month. In this particular month on this particular day, God wants to lead some of his people to another location, either physically or spiritually or both. Be alert and take advantage of his prompting and leading. It could be a great time to get that new beginning in a new location. In verse 29, Moses confirms this when he mentions that they are going to the place God had promised. God could fulfill many promises about new locations and new spiritual levels at this time, so be aware that he could be leading you to them.

In verse 35, Moses asks the Lord to rise up and let his enemies be scattered and let them flee before him. This twentieth day of the second month is a great time for God to begin to scatter your enemies, who are really *his* enemies. Believe that he is putting confusion into the plans of your enemies and that they will fight each other, just like he did with Jonathan in 1 Sam. 14:20 and Jehoshaphat in 2 Chronicles 20:23. Because of their bravery, God wins the battle for both Jonathan and Jehoshaphat. They do little and God did the rest. They just have to be obedient and go toward the enemy without retreating. This twentieth day of the second month is such a great time to take God at his Word and face your enemy, with victory assured.

In 2 Chronicles 3:2, Solomon starts to build the temple on the second day of the second month. This is a great time to start building what God has promised. Take advantage of God's timing and anointing on particular days and months of the year. Do you realize that years later, Ezra starts rebuilding the temple in the same month that Solomon started building the temple originally (Ezra 3:8)? This is truly amazing! God has everything timed out. God could have you start new foundation courses at this time to build up people's lives. This month is also a time when adversaries could begin to attack the plan God gave you for building. In Ezra 4:1, the adversaries to God's people get all riled up and made threats to attempt to stop the work. Don't be alarmed. "Greater is God that is in you than he that is in the world" (1 John 4:4). "No weapon of the enemy formed against you will prosper" (Isaiah 54:17).

Let's summarize the importance of the second month as a whole:

1. Great time to go to spiritual battle and take an inventory of who around you is capable of fighting alongside you.

2. Time to position more prayer support around yourself.

3. Great time to receive new revelations from God which could be entrances to new spiritual levels.

A summary of the importance of specific days during the month:

1. Second day- Great time to start building the structure God enabled you to build.

2. Twentieth day- Great time for God to scatter your enemies, who are really *his* enemies. Great time to move to new locations (physically or spiritually) if God directs.

During this second month, God will reveal more about the meaning of the number two in the Word. When God calls someone, he always has somebody else ready if one says no. He always has a ram in the bush. In the Old Testament, two goats were used in a sacrifice, one was killed, and the other was sent out into the wilderness. The number two represents you and me responding to an invitation from God to do something. We can either say yes or no. Again, if you say no, he always has someone else who will say yes.

In Matthew 24:40, the Word says there will be "two in the field, and one will be taken and one left." In Mark 11:4, the Word mentions that there was a colt tied where two ways met. One can go either of two ways—obey God or not. This truth about the number two is brought out in the story of the prodigal son, who leaves his father while the other son stays to do his father's will. In Genesis 2:15, man (Adam) is chosen to do a work, and in verse 18, a helpmate (Eve) is created.

In Proverbs 2:2, God is showing the importance of doing what God said by understanding the fear of the Lord. In verse 16, God talks about not letting a stranger keep you from doing what God wants, or he will have to use and bless someone else who will do what he says. In Psalm 2:11, the Psalmist says to serve the Lord with fear and rejoice with trembling. When he calls you to an assignment, make sure you accomplish it. In Jeremiah 2:7, God talks about bringing Israel into a plentiful country to eat the fruit and goodness but not to defile the land when entering. In verse 13, the Word even says two evils have been committed by his people. In verse 17, he talks about forsaking the Lord when he led them. These are warnings to you and me to obey him and not miss his blessing.

In Matthew 2:16, Herod slays all the children two years old and younger after the wise men don't do what he says. In Mark 2:14, Jesus calls Matthew and says,

"Follow me." The choice is yours to follow him and be blessed or to miss out.

The number two in the Word also means you are not doing the assignment alone, but God is with you. In Mark 2:15, Jesus sits at a meal with Matthew after he called him. He took care of him. In Matthew 2:20, God shows his protection of Joseph, Mary, and Jesus by sending them into Egypt for protection from the baby slayings ordered by Herod and providing them with gifts that were given by the wise men to support them. He'll do the same for you, for when he calls you to do something, he goes with you, blessing and sustaining you. In Jeremiah 2:7, he mentions how he called Israel into a plentiful country. Oh how wonderful his sustaining power is when he calls us!

Expect God to confirm these truths to you during this second month and walk in the awareness that he will go with you in what he calls you to do. He also wants to remind you periodically during the month that if you say no to what he is asking you to do, he always has somebody else who will say yes. This is a very important month for you to stay close to God and not pay attention to what your flesh may be saying concerning the assignment he gave you. Carry through on your assignment!

THIRD MONTH

Sivan (May-June)

In 2 Chronicles 14:9, the Word records that Asa, who was a good king, goes into battle against 1,300,000 of the enemy and God wins a great victory for his people. In 15:10, the Word declares that Asa calls all his people together in the third month. They offer a great sacrifice to God in thanksgiving for all his victories which he wrought for them. When they got together, they make a covenant with God to follow him after they had backslid earlier. God honors his part of the covenant by giving them rest from their enemies (verse 15).

This month is a great time to come back to Jesus and re-dedicate everything to him and praise him for all his past victories for you. This month is also a great time for God to demonstrate his power, especially when the odds are against you. In your situation, you may feel like 1,300,000 people are coming against you, but take this to heart—everything and everybody report to God. "All things were created by God and for God and by him all things consist"(Colossians 1:16,17). God controls everything and he gets the most glory when he wins for you with the odds stacked against you.

In 2 Chronicles 15:16, in the third month (verse 10), Asa removes his mother from being queen because she made an idol in the grove. He also cuts down and destroys the idol. This month is such a great time to separate yourself from the wrong influence in your life, even if it may be a family member. Don't let the people who are continually breaking God's commandments be an influence in your life.

How many politicians hire people just because they are relatives or because they are backers to whom they owe favors? They may be doing something illegal, and it is a case of *guilty by association*. As a result, this month is a great time to reevaluate the people who have a direct or indirect influence in your life. This reevaluation will help you avoid some potential pitfalls in your life and make you sharper in the future concerning the people you may allow to get close to you.

Especially during this month, make sure you don't have an idol in your life (i.e. somebody or something that you are putting ahead of God in terms of affection). An idol could be a person, TV program, the Internet, money, possessions, beauty (the body), power, fame, psychics, cults, etc. God may be moving, especially during this month, to remove anything or anybody that would potentially separate you from God.

It is recorded in verse 19 of this chapter of 2 Chronicles that after Asa does these things, there was no more war. When you do the things mentioned above, Satan has less legal ground in your life to work with.

In 2 Chronicles 31:1, it is recorded that Hezekiah destroys all the idols in the groves and the high altars. As a result, offerings come in for the priests and the Levites in such a great amount that they are piled in high heaps. These offerings started coming in the third month and continue until the seventh month (verse 7). What abundance! Do you see what can happen as you cast the idols and sin out of your life, especially in this third month? Abundance comes as a result of this obedience. Again, these offerings were for the priests and the Levites (the preachers). Some of you ministers reading this book may feel dry financially. But, get ready for this third month abundance as you obey his commands.

The time of Firstfruits starts on Nissan 16 and ends fifty days later on the feast of Pentecost (Sivan 6) (Leviticus 23:10–16). The appointed feast prepares us for Pentecost (Leviticus 23:16–22), which is a promotion, or explosion, time. This is a period of time when so many ministries after the season of Firstfruits can start to take off, or explode, by Pentecost. If they can allow God to deal with them during that fifty days and open themselves up to the searching of the Holy Spirit, they can be put in position on Pentecost, for their promotion.

During the time of Firstfruits, he is removing all the excess baggage so you can cross over during the season of Pentecost. This is why it is so important to know God's seasons: how he is moving and what he expects us to do. The season of Firstfruits is not a season of asking for things, but a period of time where he can prepare you for things you may start receiving on Pentecost. Again, Firstfruits is a season of finding out what is not right in our lives by the searchlight of the Holy Spirit. As we yield these areas of our lives to him, he removes them once and for all. Then we are ready for that wonderful time of Pentecost where he has prepared us to receive abundantly. Praise him! This is why so many Christians don't receive from God. They don't adapt to his seasons.

The original Pentecost on Mount Sinai was also a marriage contract that God makes with Israel (Jeremiah 2:1–3). God also makes a betrothal contract with his church body (2 Corinthians 11:2). Jew and Gentile are espoused (betrothed) to Jesus and will soon become his "wife" (Rev. 19:7–8). This season is also a time where God can bring ordained couples together for marriage.

He can arrange for divine encounters. Those of you who are single and have had a promise from God concerning marriage should be attentive for a move of God in this area at this time of year. God could start to bring that God ordained companion into your life at the start of this season.

Another aspect of the Day of Pentecost is the fact that during this feast, two loaves of bread were being offered in the temple. The two loaves represent the church comprised of Jew and Gentile alike, both born into Jesus the Messiah. Look at the start of this feast for God to pour out a special anointing to bring Jews and Gentiles closer together. Be aware, be open, and be available for him to start accomplishing this through you.

Seek him during the season of Firstfruits and get ready for some of the biggest blessings and opportunities you have ever seen. When God is in a blessing season like Pentecost, there is no telling what and how much he will pour out. It all has to do with his timing. He blesses us every day, but he still has seasons where he has overwhelming blessings and promotions.

We need to learn and take advantage of God's movement during his seasons and not try to force him to adapt to our period of expectation. As we spend time in his presence, especially during the time of Unleavened Bread and Firstfruits, we will see what is expected of us, and we can be in such a mode of receiving during such a season as Pentecost.

Let's summarize the importance of the third month:

1. Re-dedication to Jesus and remembering all his victories on our behalf.

2. He wins for you, in the face of impossible odds.

3. Remove the people in your life who could be influencing you away from God, directly or indirectly.

A summary of the importance of specific days during the month:

1. The sixth day- Pentecost anointing for empowerment and promotion. Also, people who had an advantage over you now lose their advantage. This time of the month is also a time of positioning by God.

There is a general anointing on this third month for God to show you he is with you and that he is God of anything you are going through for him. This is one of the meanings of the use of the number three in the Word. He demonstrates his many attributes in this month more than any other. In this month, God confirms that he is with you and encourages you.

Let's look together at some of the books of the Bible and see the truth about the number three and how it can affect your life. We will look at situations in the word where the number three is mentioned.

In Genesis 6:9, the Word says that Noah walks with God and this was confirmed by the next verse. In verse 10, the Word says that Noah has three sons. This is God showing Noah that he is going with him. He is going with you too!

In Genesis 15:5, Abraham is told by God that he would be the father of many nations. In verse 9, after Abraham asks God for a sign that this would happen, God tells him to take a heifer, goat and a ram of three years old and lay it before him. This was showing by the number three that God would make sure that he would bring forth the promise of a son through his bowels. Again, God can do the impossible in your life too, as you get him directly involved by turning the situation over to him. God again confirmed this in Genesis 18:2 where three angels come to Abraham and God confirms through these angels what he promised before about Abraham's seed. Sarah makes three measures of fine meal for the three angels (verse 6). The fact that there are three angels and three measures of meal signify that God would do what he said he would do (Abraham and Sarah having a son of their own). This is evident in verse 14, where God asked the question "Is there anything too hard for God?" The mention of the number three means that God will see to it that his promise will be done. This is a promise for you and I also; "Is there anything too hard for God?"

In the book of Exodus, 10:22, Moses stretches forth his rod and there is darkness three days in Egypt. This use of the number three signifies that God would take them out of Egypt and his presence would go with them as also seen in chapter 33:14–15. In Leviticus 19:23, God tells them that when they shall come into the new land that they should plant fruit trees and not eat of the fruit on them for three years. The use of the number three again is signifying that God would take them into their new land. You too!

In Numbers 12:4, God requests that three people come unto him in the tabernacle (Moses, Aaron, and Miriam). This was God again reaffirming his promise to go with them and lead them into the promised land! In Deuteronomy 16:16, God tells the Israelites that three times in the year all males should appear before him (Feast of Tabernacles, Unleavened Bread, and the Feast of Weeks). Again, this was signifying the fact that he would take them into the new land. Keeping these three feasts signifies that he would bring them in.

In Joshua 1:11, God tells the people that in three days they would cross over the Jordan River into the promise land. God's word is always true. If he said that he would bring you in, he will.

Remember, during the third month, God is confirming that he is God over whatever you are facing and that he will be with you to carry you through. Let him show forth his many attributes in your life during this month.

FOURTH MONTH

Tammuz (June- July)

In Jeremiah 39:14, after the Babylonians conquered Jerusalem, Jeremiah is delivered from prison (his people didn't listen to his prophecy and threw him into prison). This happens in the fourth month (verse 2). The king, Zedekiah, who also didn't listen to Jeremiah, is thrown into prison after his sons are slain right before his eyes. Also, his eyes are plucked out (verses 6–8). He takes Jeremiah's place in prison. As a result, this is a great month for God to confirm the word he gave you for others, even though they wouldn't listen. He can also deliver you from any plans that they may have against you. He may put your enemies and the people who wouldn't listen to the word God gave you for them into the same situation they had devised against you. The tables might be turned.

In Ezekiel 1, the Lord shows a vision to Ezekiel of four creatures joined to each other and going in the same direction, guided by the Spirit of God. He also sees them determined to continue in the direction the Spirit of God leads them (verses 4–12). This vision occurs on the fifth day of the fourth month. This is a great time for God to put things in or back into order. He can give fresh direction or confirm direction already given. This is a time where he wants to raise up teams with one God-given purpose and no big egos. This time is an excellent time to send out teams for important assignments.

You have correctly waited for the right time to put your plan into effect and this is one of the times during the year where God says, "Push out from the shore or take off." He has been assembling the team and they are now ready. Don't wait too long to do so because all of God's windows of opportunity do close eventually. The fire of the Holy Ghost is on these teams (verse 13). These teams will make a lot of noise in the devil's territory (v. 24).

As recorded in Zechariah 8:19, God talks about the fast of the fourth month as a fast of joy. It is a time for celebration, so celebrate with the Lord. Have a Holy Ghost party. Celebrate what he has done or will do, by faith. Drive the devil crazy with the noise of the party. God also mentions, as recorded in verses 20–21, that multitudes will come your way. Believe for increase in ministry, business, anointing, etc. This is truly a time of joy. It is a time where God will make up for the times of sadness. Praise him!

Let's summarize the importance of the fourth month as a whole:

1. God confirming the word that he gave you for others, who didn't pay heed.

2. God reverses the plans of the people who refused to believe the word you had for them.

3. Celebration of what God has done or will do and another great time for godly increase.

A summary of the importance of specific days during the month:

1. Fifth Day- Time for God to send out

> teams that will follow his leading, in one accord. They will have the fire of the Holy Ghost and make a lot of noise in the devil's territory.

The number four in the Word stands for the earth. There are four seasons and four directions (north, east, south, and west). Your attack is on the earth and he will give you victory on the earth. In this fourth month especially, God is telling you that since the attack is affecting you in the natural, he is about to give you victory in the natural. God knows we exist in the natural and we need to be blessed in this arena too. He just wants our souls to prosper first (3 John 2). He is about to prepare a table in the midst of your enemies (Psalm 23:5). He also says that in nothing shall you be ashamed (Romans 10:11). The very area that the enemy is attacking is the very area that God is ready to bless you in this month. Job got blessed double after his trial.

Let's look at the use of the number four in the Word by looking at some chapters and verses with the number four: "The earth is God's and the fullness thereof" (Psalm 24:1).

In Mark 4:1–23, Jesus talks about the seed in the earth, showing us that we are his seed in the earth and that we will bring forth much fruit here. In verse 28, Jesus talks about the earth again as he mentions that our blessings come on the earth as a blade, then an ear, then a full corn in the ear. When you see the blade of your miracle, the little cloud the size of a man's hand, then you need to rejoice! Your victory is near, right on the earth. In verses 35–41, he shows us his power over the things of the earth by calming the sea. He can do it for you right where you are, right on the earth.

This truth about the number four is further evident

in Daniel 3:25, where Nebuchadnezzar sees four in the fiery furnace. This means to you that nothing on earth (number four), nor anything in the natural, can separate you from God. He also will deliver you from any fiery furnace that may be against you on the earth!

In Acts 12:4, Peter is delivered to four *quaternions* of soldiers to be guarded in prison (four squads of four soldiers each). As you can see from verses 7–11, the number four in this chapter in verse 4 means that nothing on earth can keep Peter in prison. God sets him free and leads him out! He promises to do the same for you, especially during this fourth month.

In Acts 27:29, Paul is on a ship going toward Rome and a great storm comes against the ship. They cast four anchors and are fearful. In chapter 28, Paul is delivered from the storm and is taken to the destination God had purposed for him (Acts 28:30–31). Nothing on earth (number four) could stop him.

In Exodus 25:12, Moses is told by God to put four rings of gold on the Ark of the Covenant in the tabernacle. Jesus is our ark of safety, our God (gold) who came on the earth (number four) to save us from our sins. Nothing on earth could stop him, nor can anything stop you from getting where God wants you to go. God will especially bless you during this fourth month. Expect!

FIFTH MONTH

Av (July-Aug.)

In Jeremiah 52:12, the Word says the enemy invades and takes Jerusalem on the tenth day of the fifth month. This is a time to be on guard to a greater degree for the attack of the enemy. I don't want you to be devil-conscious, but listen carefully to the Spirit of God as he warns.

On the same day of the same month in Ezekiel 20, God tells his people to remember how their ancestors rebelled against him and his ways and worshiped idols. He pleads with them not to make the same mistake. He also mentions that he wants to bring them into land he promised them. He is saying the same thing today, especially during this month (i.e. forsake any idols and obey his statutes).

His sword is ready to strike. We need to go back with the Holy Spirit and allow him to bring to mind the sins of our ancestors, ask him to forgive them, break any curses, replace our ungodly beliefs with godly beliefs, and allow him to remove any and all spirit/soul hurts from the past. He wants an opportunity to clean up our past and get our attention off of people and onto him. He wants to remove any and all idols.

He also mentions in verse 38 that he wants to remove the rebels from amongst them. He wants to do the same thing today, especially at this time of the year. He wants to remove those people in your life who are rebelling against him and might be causing you to do the same.

Believe that God will bring those negative influences out of your children's lives at the same time. There is a special anointing to do so at this time. He says in verses 42 and 44 that if we do the above mentioned concerning the sins of our ancestors, he will then bring us into our land of inheritance for his mercies' sake. Wow! Take advantage of his mercy.

In Ezra 7:8, the Word mentions that Ezra arrives at Jerusalem in the fifth month after traveling three months from Babylon to rebuild the temple of God. He arrives at his purpose at last. This could be the time that you arrive at your purpose. Be on the alert; your purpose could be right in front of you and be revealed at this time of the year.

At the time of his arrival in Jerusalem to rebuild the temple, he has in his possession all he needed to finish the job. Artaxerxes, the king of Babylon, had given him gold and silver to use in whatever way he deemed fit for rebuilding the temple of God. He also gave a letter ordering treasurers in the area along the way to do the same if he didn't have enough. Artaxerexes commanded that all the money would be tax-free (verse 24). Can you believe for the same favor to do your purpose?

There is a special anointing on this time of the year for this favor. God will touch people's hearts to do this in your life. All the people Ezra needs to help him do his purpose are there and in place (verse 28). Please take advantage of this season and expect provision for the vision.

Also, as I mentioned in the chapter on the fourth month, the Lord set aside certain months for celebration as recorded in Zechariah 8:19. Besides the fourth month, he also set aside this month. So rejoice in the Lord for what he has done and will do for you. Believe for increase as blessings, people, and opportunities start coming your way (verse 21–23).

In Jeremiah 28:1, in the fifth month, the false prophet Hananiah mentions that God would break the yoke of the king of Babylon, and within two years all that the enemy took would be returned to his people. He didn't believe Jeremiah's prophecy that the king of Babylon would conquer them and keep them in captivity for seventy years. He tries to contradict his prophecy with a false one. God speaks through Jeremiah that this false prophet would die within a year, which happens.

This is also a time for judgment on the false prophets who have led God's people astray. God cares too much for his people to continue to allow the false prophets to continue, especially if they don't repent. A prophecy is special and personal. People open their spirits to prophecy and he doesn't want his people hurt.

Let's summarize the importance of the fifth month as a whole:

1. Be ready! Expect all the provisions for the vision he has given you to start coming from people he brings into your life.

2. Joyous celebration during this month.

3. Time of punishment of false prophets who refuse to repent.

A summary of the importance of specific days during the month:

1. Tenth day- Be on guard for a possible major attack from the enemy. Go back with the Holy Spirit and let him get rid of the effect of past events in your life and the lives of your ancestors.

The number five stands for God coming into your trial redeeming, restoring, and strengthening you, in order for you to arrive where he wants you to go in him. During this fifth month is when God personally wants to come to refresh you. This is when you need his refreshment the most. During this month is when he wants to walk into your situation (trial) and not only refresh you, but let you know that he will take you the rest of the way. He wants to give you strength to continue onto the rest of the trial.

In the gospel of John, chapter 5, verses 1–9, there is a pool with five porches and there is a man who had an infirmity for thirty-eight years. Jesus comes and heals him (verse 9). He will do the same for you right now, if you believe. Believe and receive your healing right now in Jesus' name!

In Mark 5:1–17, Jesus comes to the country of the Galdarenes and sets a man free who is filled with demons. He can do the same for you now. Believe and receive your deliverance right now in the name of Jesus! Later, in verse 41, Jesus raises Jarius's daughter from the dead after coming to her house. He can come where you are and raise up whatever is dead in your life.

In Luke 5:2, there is a picture of fishermen who had finished fishing and were cleaning their nets. To them this was not a time to fish. Here is another situation where Jesus is coming on the scene to help a situation that seemed hopeless. They allow Jesus to use their boat for his purposes, and he then fills their boat with fish. He'll do the same for you. Do his business, and he will get into your business and bless it. He can fill and bless you to overflowing. Take advantage of this and move with him during this last of the last times.

In Matthew 5:1, Jesus sees that the people needed

something. He comes to them and shows them truths they need (the Beatitudes). He shows them important truths on how to attract his anointing and blessings in their lives by his Beatitude teaching. So believe during this fifth month that Jesus is coming your way to strengthen and encourage you during your trial. It may seem hopeless, but he is coming. All things were created by him and for him and by him all things consist. Everything and everybody is under his control. Praise him.

SIXTH MONTH

Elul (Aug.-Sept.)

In Haggai 1:1–9, in the sixth month on the first day of the month, the Lord admonishes his people. He said, "You all have your house, what about mine?" They are going through a period of no rain, a drought because they are not obeying him. He tells them to build his house. He also mentions in verse 13 that he was with them and they would not be building alone.

At this time of the year, God is saying to us to step out by faith and do what he asked us to do. If he asked you to build something for him, start building. Some of you already have the land, now build. He already brought you to this point in your life; now carry through on what he has asked you to do. He doesn't only mean to build something physically. He may be asking you at this time to start stepping out in ministry. When you do, he will start shaping and building your ministry, but you have to step out first. Abraham leaves where he was and goes into a new land, in order to be blessed (Hebrews 11:8–10).

In Haggai 1:14–15, the Word says that on the twenty-fourth day of this month, God starts stirring up helpers for this work. He'll do the same for you. Again step out in faith. You will be so surprised about whom God will call to help. He will also call people with means to help finance the work. Don't take on the burden of building by yourself.

During this month, the season of Teshuvah occurs. The season of Teshuvah is a call to repentance. Repentance means more than turning from one's sins; it is a return to God and to the right path. Teshuvah begins on Elul 1, the first day of the sixth month. The season of Teshuvah is a time for each person to examine his own life. It is also a time to restore relationships with other people. It is a continuation of the Feast of Unleavened Bread and Firstfruits in the sense of self-examination and being conformed to the image of Jesus.

Teshuvah is a forty-day season which starts on Elul 1 and ends on Yom Kippur, which is ten days after Rosh HaShannah (Feast of Trumpets). God always has a special season of repentance before a season of a mighty move of promotion. The season of Teshuvah is no exception. The season that this time of Teshuvah is preparing one for is Rosh HaShannah, or the Feast of Trumpets, which occurs in the seventh month.

God's promotion, for the most part, only comes in certain seasons. This is why it is so important to recognize the seasons of preparation for promotion, breakthrough, and other rich blessings. Praise him!

This time is also a season of making sure that one is right with God, or born again. During a Feast of Trumpets, or Rosh HaShannah, in the future is when Jesus is coming back for us in the Rapture. This is why Teshuvah is so important: to make sure that one is right with God by being born again. It is also important for those who are born again to draw closer to Jesus and continue to allow God to change them into the image of his Son during this season.

In Ezekiel 8:1, Ezekiel says in the fifth day of the sixth month that he sees a vision from God. In verse 7, the Word says that God shows him a hole in the wall of his sanctuary. He sees idols painted on the walls and people doing abominable things in his sanctuary. In verse 14, Ezekiel sees women weeping for Tammuz, the son of Seminaris, a pagan Queen from Babylon. In verse 16, the Word says that God shows even worse abominations (i.e. twenty-five men worshiping the sun). God says in verse 18 that he was going to deal with them in his fury.

At this time of the year, God is pouring out his same wrath on some in his church who are committing abominations. How many pastors treat their people (really, *God's* people) as if they are cattle that have been branded with their denominational mark? They see dollar signs over their heads. They get so upset if God calls some of their members to visit another congregation, especially if that congregation is not part of their denomination. They are jealous, covetous, and greedy. God is about to pour out his wrath on them at this time. Just watch! This is the same righteous anger that came on Jesus in driving out the money-changers in the temple, his house.

In Luke 1:26, the Word says that the angel Gabriel is sent to Mary the mother of Jesus in the sixth month. He announces to her that the Holy Spirit would overshadow her and that she would bear a son, who would be the Son of the Highest. At this time of the year, the Holy Spirit wants to overshadow all your fears, worries, incapabilities, and low esteem and plant a seed of purpose in you. He wants to overshadow your past and do a marvelous work in you that he can bring out of you at a later time in order to bless others.

Later on, Mary goes to her cousin Elizabeth's house, and Elizabeth recognizes that God has blessed her and speaks a promise into her life. Others will recognize that God has done a work in you at this time of the year. In verses 46–49, the Word says that this is when she conceives as the Holy Spirit overshadows her body, soul, and spirit. He couldn't do it where Joseph was located. This is why she had to leave and go to Elizabeth's house.

This time of the year, God may ask you to leave situations, relationships, positions, etc., in order to get blessed. Be alert! He wants you alone in his presence, in order for him to overshadow and bless you. There may be a gentle but powerful drawing on you to come into his presence that you never felt before. This is the reason: that he may conceive a work or a vision in you that many will recognize and be blessed by. Mary says in verse 48 that all generations will call her blessed.

Let's summarize the importance of the sixth month as a whole:

1. Time for God to overshadow your past, incapabilities, worries, etc., and plant something in your spirit that will bless many.

A summary of the importance of specific days during the month:

1. First day- Time to step out and let God build a ministry around you. This is a time for some to physically build what he is asking you to construct. He will also bring the workers to help. Time of the season called Teshuvah. This is a time for repentance and returning to the old paths.

2. Fifth day- God will bring great judgment and wrath on some in his church for their idols and abominations at this time.

There is a general anointing on this sixth month for

God to bring someone into your life to bless you and help you with your destiny. Also at this time, the enemy may try to use an individual to come against you in a greater way.

The number six in the Word is the number for man. Man was created on the sixth day. It has a great meaning for us during this month. At this time, the devil would like to use a person—man, woman, boy, or girl—to come against you, to talk you into giving up, or to try to hinder you. Sometimes it could be the person closest to you whom Satan may try to use. Be alert during this month. You need to keep your focus on Jesus and resist what the devil is trying to do through that person. Jesus wants you to keep your eyes on him and not man, especially in a trial. There is so much at stake.

In Mark 6:1–6, men come against Jesus with unbelief and Jesus can do no mighty work there (verse 5). Satan wants man to interfere with your work for God by trying to bring unbelief your way. They might ask, "Did God really say that to you?" They may try to put the blame on you if you are going through a trial, like Job's friends did.

In Nehemiah 6, the Word says Nehemiah is leading people to rebuild the wall of Jerusalem. Sanbellat and Tobiah try to get him to come down (verse 2). In verse 3, Nehemiah says he is doing a great work and will not come down. This is a prime example of people trying to get you to give up on what God told you to do and escape the trial you are going through.

God can also send somebody to bless you during this month, so be observant. During this sixth month, at the very least, expect the activity of more people into your life, one way or another.

Please remember during this sixth month especially that you need to cut off any influence man has on you to turn you away from God's purpose. Remember to look for God to use somebody to bless you too.

SEVENTH MONTH

Tishrei (Sept.-Oct.)

In Jeremiah 28, a false prophet by the name of Hananiah is telling the Israelites that whatever and whomever the Babylonians had taken from the Israelites would be returned within two years (verse 11). Jeremiah rebukes him and tells him he will die because he was falsely leading the people (verses 12–17). He dies in the same year in the seventh month. He had prophesized falsely in the fifth month (verse 1) and was killed two months later. Sometimes God's justice and punishment are swift.

There is a special anointing on this seventh month to expose and rebuke the false prophets who only want to prophesy what people want to hear. They also want to prophesy things that would benefit themselves when they speak well of the other person. If the person they are ministering to has money, they want to manipulate a "prophecy" to benefit themselves and get some of their money.

This is a time when God wants to cut off their influence on unsuspecting saints. Some prophets only prophesy to profit. They may seem to be getting away with something because justice may seem to be delayed, but no. God's punishment is always on time. God says in Ezekiel 14:9 that he will destroy the false prophets from the midst of his people. These false prophets fail to realize that the people they are ministering to are God's children and they need to be careful. No human father would permit anybody to mistreat his children, much less God.

In Jeremiah 41:1–2, in the seventh month, Gedaliah, even though he was warned by Ishmael of a plot to kill him, rejects this warning and is killed. Some saints need to be careful during this month especially, and watch for the devil to try to take back promotions and blessings God has bestowed. Resist the devil and go on with your work for Jesus, but be watchful for a retaliation attack by Satan to try to take back ground God has given to you. Don't be overconfident at a victory: stand guard. The time period right after a victory is the most dangerous time for some people as they might let down their guard.

In Haggai 2:1, the Word of the Lord came to Haggai in the seventh month on the twentieth day, and he encourages Zerubbabel and Joshua to start the work of rebuilding the temple of God in Jerusalem. He tells them not to fear and that he is with them (verses 4–5) in this work.

He is saying the same thing to his people at the same time of this month. "Be strong, for I am with you to start and complete the work I have placed on your heart. If you just take a step in the direction I told you to go, and don't look back or doubt, I will enable you to finish my assignment." This is a word for you and me today. Sure, he can initiate a work at any time during the year, but there is a special anointing on this day and month. It doesn't matter who stands in your way; they all report to God and have to bow to his wishes.

God also speaks to Haggai in verse 7 that he will bring people to help him in the work, and in verse 8, he says that all the gold and silver is his. He is telling Haggai that not only would he bring the people to help and be a part of this work, but that he would finance everything.

The same promise is for you and me, so claim it with me. You don't need to borrow from the world to build the building God asked you to build, but trust him to bring the finances and the workers. Oh how great is his favor!

God confirms this promise in Zechariah 8:19–23. He says that this seventh month would be a time of joy and feasting. He also says he would cause people to come to the temple, seeking him and his presence. God is not setting you up in your own building and ministry to fail, but that so many would come your way to find him. Just make sure he is with and behind you and approves your purpose. This is an excellent time of the year for him to confirm his approval. God won't bring the people to see you, but to draw closer and find him.

Rosh HaShannah, or the Feast of Trumpets, is truly a season of a new beginning. This feast occurs on the first day of the seventh month. It is a two-day feast. This feast is thirty days after Teshuvah and ten days before Yom Kippur. According to many Jewish teachers, the day of trumpets involves the sounding of the last trump. The last trump is a blast of the Shofar (a trumpet made from a curved ram's horn) that is blown on this day.

When Abraham was told to sacrifice Isaac, a ram was caught in the thicket. The left horn was called the first trump and the right horn, the last trump. The first trump was blown on the original Pentecost on Mount Sinai (Exodus 19:13). The last trump will be blown on the last day of a particular Feast of Trumpets in the future, when Jesus returns to take us in the Rapture. This season reminds us that he is coming for us on some future day on this feast and to be ready.

In 2 Thessalonians 2:3, the Word says there will be a falling away before the day of the Lord. The phrase *day of Lord* refers to the seven-year tribulation period and the millennium period of one thousand years after the end of the tribulation. I believe the phrase *falling away* is a mistranslation of the Greek word *apostasia* and should be translated *departure*. The root verb of this word is *aphistemi*, which is found fifteen times in the New Testament. It is translated *depart* eleven times. Although it is often found translated in similar meanings, the predominant meaning of this verb is the act of a person departing from another person or from a place. I believe the correct rendering of this *apostasia*, in the context of Paul's Greek word, means a departure and not any kind of falling away. His context is not revealing any kind of apostasy, but instead, teaching concerning the coming of Jesus for his saints. This verse shows that the Rapture will occur before the tribulation period.

Paul described this event in 1 Thessalonians 4:17. "Then we which are alive and remain shall be caught-up together with them in the clouds to meet the Lord in the air," which then proves that this event involves a departure from the earth. Another word we need to look at in the Greek is the word *caught-up* in this verse (I Thess. 4:17). This Greek word is *harpuzo*, meaning *to catch away*. Its Hebrew equivalent is the word *natzal*, which in its root form, means *to deliver*.

Those who don't go in the Rapture will face a seven-year time of the wrath of God, tribulation, and indignation. So every celebration of Rosh HaShannah points to a particular Rosh HaShannah, or Feast of Trumpets, in the future when Jesus comes back for us. Also, every celebration of this feast warns us to be ready for this great event. Every season of Rosh HaShannah is a wonderful anointed time where God can bring about a new beginning in your life and promote. You need to take advantage of the time of Teshuvah (starts thirty days prior) to prepare for Rosh HaShannah. We need to expect God to take us higher and higher in his anointing during Rosh HaShannah. We talked earlier about the beginning of the year on Nisan 1 (our March-April time period) in the section on the "First Month." Rosh HaShannah is another attempt by God to give people a new beginning. This time is the civil New Year to many Jews, as opposed to the religious New Year of Nisan 1. It is so important to adapt to God's seasons and to do what is necessary, at the right time, to receive his blessings that are reserved mostly for the particular season you are in.

Yom Kippur (Day of Atonement), on the tenth day in the seventh month, is ten days after Rosh HaShannah and ends the forty days of Teshuvah. This feast, when it was celebrated originally, was a temporal atonement and redemption. The great tribulation will start ten days after the Rapture (which occurs on Tishri 1, or Rosh HaShannah), on Tishri 10, which is the Day of Atonement. The Great Tribulation will end seven years later on the Day of Atonement, and it will also be the day of the second coming of Jesus.

This is a time where believers who are feeling oppressed and surrounded by enemies can take solace that Jesus is coming to deliver. This is a great day of deliverance. Jesus can surely deliver any day of the year, but this is a special day to meet the need of deliverance. Believers who need deliverance in any area of their lives should take advantage of the special anointing on this day. During this time we need to instruct people to reach out with extra faith and receive their deliverance, no matter how long they have been oppressed.

Remember that the oppression of the Great Tribulation will end on Yom Kippur, the Day of Atonement. People who are on earth during the seven years of the Tribulation and come to Jesus will be delivered from the oppression of the antichrist. Praise him! Every previous Day of Atonement before the one that starts the Great Tribulation announces the start of a period where God is going to unleash a season of wrath onto the earth, in order to warn people to repent. This is evidenced by the Great Tribulation starting on the Day of Atonement.

One of the best ways to avoid giving into the spirit of the antichrist and going through the Tribulation is to study and meditate on what Jesus said to the churches in Revelation chapters 2 and 3. What Jesus spoke to the churches in Revelation 2 and 3 is to prepare saints for the Rapture, where Jesus will take his saints away with him, before the great tribulation. This is evident in Revelation 4:1, where Jesus uses the term "Come up hither." It is important to see if we fall short and can identify with any of the warnings to his churches in chapters 2 and 3. Be careful that you haven't left your first love, Jesus. This is just one of the warnings to his church. Stay away from pride and self.

The Feast of Tabernacles starts on the fifteenth day in the seventh month and ends on the twenty-second day. In Leviticus 23:33–34, God reveals the establishment of his appointed time called *Sukkot*, or Tabernacles. This appointed time commemorates the time when Israel traveled in the wilderness as God led them. During this time, God lived with his people in his own tabernacle. He also provided a cloud of covering that shaded the people by day and a cloud of fire to warm his people by night.

Just what does this feast mean for us? I feel that one of the meanings of this season is that this is a time where God will give fresh direction in ministries and start moving them toward some uncharted areas. This is a season where the new direction he was preparing you for will start to come into view. Again, this is a wonderful season to step out as he leads. He may anoint some of his people to change locations. This is a time where God will clear out obstacles in the way of his people in order for them to move, much like one would clear out brush going through a jungle. This is a time when God will make a change of locations smoother than one could ever imagine. Just like he moved his people out of Egypt, he tells some of his people to move now! He creates an opening that one needs to take complete advantage of. This is definitely a time to stay up with the moving of the Holy Spirit and take advantage of his window of opportunity. This also a time where all the preparations he put you through pay off as release happens.

Also, this feast is also known as the Feast of Nations. During this festival, seventy sacrifices were offered with each being understood as a representation of each of the seventy nations of the known world at that time.

Another key truth of this festival is the use of the number seven. A fascinating thing about the sacrifices during Tabernacles is that when the offerings were grouped together or counted, their number always remains divisible by seven. During the week of Tabernacles, or Sukkot, there are 182 sacrifices (70 bullocks, 14 rams, and 98 lambs, divides by 7 into 182 exactly 26 times). Add to this the grain offerings, 336 tenths of ephahs of flour (48 x 7) (Numbers 29:12–40). This use of the number seven, which means completion, is that God wants to complete some things he started in your life during this season. God is a God of fulfillment. "Being confident of this very thing, that he which hath begun a good work in you will perform it until the day of Jesus Christ" (Philippians 1:6).

Another theme for the appointed time of Sukkot is called The Festival of Ingathering. This time of year marks the times of the harvest, the final ingathering of all produce before the coming winter (Exodus 23:16). This is a time where there is a tremendous anointing being poured out by God to get people saved. Expect God to put you into key situations where there are unsaved people. You will find that God can engineer divine encounters to bring strangers into your life for the express purpose of bringing them to salvation. You will find that those whom you least expected to desire to get saved will start asking questions. Please, please, take advantage of this season.

In Zechariah 14:16–21, the Word talks about the millennium period of time, a period of one thousand years after the great tribulation period. The chapter talks about some of the effects that will take place in the lives of people who do not come to Jerusalem to keep this feast. In verses 17 and 18, the Word mentions that the ones that don't come won't have any rain. Rain speaks of refreshing and moisture for those who are dry. This is a great season of refreshment. Remember how God led and protected his people during their time in the wilderness and watch how he pours out his refreshment anointing on you. In verse 21, God says that no Canaanite will be there during this feast in Jerusalem. This is a promise to you that God can take the deceitful enemies out of your life. Claim and believe this, especially during this season.

Let's summarize the importance of the seventh month as a whole:

1. A time of punishment for false prophets.

2. A possible time of Satan trying to rob promotions.

A summary of the importance of specific days during the month:

1. First Day–Season of Rosh HaShannah, a time of new beginnings and promotion.

2. Tenth Day–Season of the Day of Atonement, a season of judgment by God, but also a time of great deliverance. The Great Tribulation will start on this feast some time in the future.

3. Fifteenth Day–Season of Tabernacles-time for God to give new direction and for one to step out boldly in this new direction. Also this season is a great time for a great harvest of souls in all nations.

4. Twentieth Day–Another time to start building a work for God. God will finance and send workers for this new work.

There is a special meaning to the number seven in the Word. The number seven means that God is about to complete something in your life. Besides the seventh hour of the day, there is an anointing in the seventh month as a whole for increased activity on God's part to complete promotions and other blessings in your life at any time during the month.

EIGHTH MONTH

Cheshvan (Oct.-Nov.)

In 1 Kings 6:38, the Word says that the temple which Solomon built for God is finished and completed in the eighth month. There is such an anointing on this month for God to complete what he started, even if the process has been going on for a long period of time and give you a new beginning. This is a great time for God to finish what he promised that he would do for you.

Expect him to wrap up lawsuits hanging out there in your favor. Look for God to move on those people who are holding onto the finances they promised you. Look for God to complete your job search with an offer of a position that fits you perfectly. Look for God to finish having your new house completed where it has been delayed and delayed. God can complete healing processes both physically and emotionally. He can complete your wilderness experiences and promote you like Moses (Exodus 3:10) and Daniel (Daniel 5:29). Look for God to complete that trial that seems to be going on so long. This is a time where you can say, *Thank God I hung in there because the ordeal is over.* This is a great time to finally receive your breakthrough or new beginning.

In 1 Kings 12:32, Jeroboam sets up a pagan feast day in the eighth month on the fifteenth day. Look for the possibility of the spirit of the antichrist to try to interfere with a move of God by demonstrating more power during this time. This spirit likes to have religious events try to cloud a true move of God. Jeroboam wanted to have his own feasts for the ten tribes up north so his people would not miss the godly feasts their brothers in the south were having. This was in conflict with the godly feasts God had instructed his people to have.

This spirit wants people to believe the false and miss the real. Don't be afraid, just be alert. An example would be that you are going to a real anointed church and somebody invites you to see a prophet who came to town. He starts speaking some condemnation into your life and sets you back on God's timetable. This is an example of the spirit of the antichrist wanting to take someone out of purpose (1 John 2:18–19). So stay focused on purpose, especially during this time to avoid this snare.

Let's summarize the importance of the eighth month as a whole:

1. A time for God to complete things in your life, to finalize situations in your favor and give you a new beginning.

A summary of the importance of specific days during the month:

1. Fifteenth Day–A time to be especially focused as the spirit of the antichrist is looking to camouflage what God is doing by doing a counterfeit work.

The number eight in the Word means that God has already spoken your new beginning that will come to you and that could happen during this eighth month. This new beginning has already been loosed.

In Genesis 8:12, Noah sends a dove out of the ark, and it does not return. God was showing him that his new beginning was just ahead of him. In v.16, this promise was for his whole family too. God is showing you during this eighth month the new beginning or level is just ahead for you and that your family is included in this blessing. In verse 5, the tops of the mountains are seen. God will at least show you a portion of your new beginning during this month.

In Exodus 8:22, God puts a division between his people and the Egyptians by saying that no plague from that point on would touch his people in Goshen. He is telling them that this is a sign of their new beginning. He is now separating them from the trials that would be coming on the Egyptians. During this month, God will be letting you know that he is now separating you from some people who want to keep you in bondage.

In Numbers 8:14, God separates the Levites from the rest of the people and says they shall be his. He gives them a sign of this new beginning by having all the children of Israel put their hands on them and pray as recorded in verse 10. During this month, God may use somebody to remind you of a promise he gave you or even give you a new promise. This is to show that there will be a new beginning in your life. Please look for it this eighth month.

NINTH MONTH

Kislev (Nov.-Dec.)

In Jeremiah 36:1–3, God gives a message of warning through Jeremiah to the people of Israel to repent and tells him to write it in a book. In the ninth month, Baruch, the servant to Jeremiah, proclaims a fast and reads all the words of the book to the people (verse 9–10). The king of Israel hears about this. He reads some of the book and burns it in the fire. The king gets angry and wants to capture Jeremiah and Baruch, but the Word says that God hides them. God really gets angry at the response of the king of Israel to his words and pronounces judgment on the king and the rest of the people (verse 27–31). He tells Jeremiah to write down the message again in a book and this time he adds to it.

This ninth month is a time of warning from God to repent, especially to some of the leadership. His warning cannot be overlooked or destroyed. This is a time for God's prophets to be more determined and obedient than ever to deliver his messages, whether they are received or not. The Body of Christ needs to be told about repentance, especially during this time. This is not the time for God's people to look to hear about their new car coming or new house. Those things are appropriate in their time. This is the time to hear God's warning about repentance and act on his words. As usual, God will also hide his true prophets at this time from any retaliation.

In Haggai 2:20–23, on the twenty-fourth day of the ninth month, God has a similar message of repentance and says that he is going to overthrow some of the leadership (verse 22). God also says in verse 23 that he is going to make Zerubbabel a signet. This is also a time of raising some of his key people to be signets or examples of the power that he can exhibit in and through one person.

This message of repentance for God's people in this month is repeated in Zechariah 7:1–14 on the fourth day of the ninth month. Also, in Chapter 8:12, God pronounces a blessing upon his remnant that they will posses all things, also in this same month. Make sure you are part of his remnant by allowing him to conform you into the image of his Son. You can then start possessing all the blessings God sends your way. Also, expect increase in people coming to your purpose or ministry as God promises in verses 21–23. As God promises in verse 23, expect that people will start recognizing that God is with you and come running toward you. God also says he will lift you up as an ensign during this same time, but he also says in Chapter 11:8 that he will cut off three pastors within thirty days. When God promotes, he "puts down one and raises up another" (Psalm 75:6–7).

In Ezra 10:9, the children of Israel gather together on the twentieth day of the ninth month and repent that they had taken strange wives from other groups of people. They put away all these strange wives. This is such a great time to allow God to remove those people who could negatively affect your walk with Jesus. (I am not advocating divorce).

Let's summarize the importance of specific days in the ninth month:

1. Fourth Day and the Twenty-Fourth Day- A period where God especially warns to repent or face judgment, especially dealing with some leadership. God especially protects his prophets who have to speak this repentance or judgment message at this time.

2. Fourth Day and the Twenty-Fourth Day- A period where God causes others to see some of his remnant as signets or examples of his power and favor. He is also putting a blessing on his remnant to possess all things.

3. Fourth Day- He is adding to ministries that his hand is on.

4. Fourth Day- He is cutting off counterfeit pastors.

5. Twentieth Day- He wants to remove people from our lives who could hinder us.

There is a general anointing on this ninth month for God to use somebody you least expect to bless you and also for the enemy to use somebody you least expect to come against you.

In Genesis 9:22, Ham sees his father's (Noah's) nakedness and is cursed. Noah probably does not expect Ham, one of his sons, to do that. Japheth and Shem, his other sons, get blessed for covering up their father (verse 26–27). God unexpectedly uses their brother's mistake to bless them!

In Exodus 9:16, God speaks of how he raises Pharaoh up to show forth his power and that his name would be declared throughout the earth. God can use somebody you don't expect to provoke you as they come against you, to bring you to a promise land of blessings. Because the Pharaoh resisted God, God had to exhibit his strength in the demonstration of his power at the Red Sea as he helped the Israelites on their journey. God used someone unexpectedly to show forth his power (Pharaoh). This was an attack but also a blessing on his people.

Again, especially during this ninth month, God can allow somebody that you least expect to come against you or to bless you. You need to be alert for either situation.

TENTH MONTH

Tevet (Dec.-Jan.)

In Jeremiah 52:4, the Word records that Nebuchadnezzar begins to invade and besiege Jerusalem on the tenth day of the tenth month. This time of the month is a time where God might deal with some of his people by having their enemies put an unusual amount of pressure on them. They may be permitted by God to come where they were not permitted before. This is a way of God pouring out his judgment on some of his people because they are not obeying him. Warn his people of this impending judgment.

God reiterates his judgment, this time to the Egyptians in Ezekiel 29:1–21, on the twelfth day of the tenth month. In 33:21, God brings judgment on his people because they set up idols (verse 25), because they only love with their mouths and not their hearts, and they go after their covetousness (verse 31). Again, this is a time to warn God's people of his possible judgment.

God also mentions that some pastors are included in his judgment in 34:2. They are not feeding the congregations but are more interested in feeding themselves. He says in verse 23 that he will replace them with a shepherd like David who will feed his people. He said he would put shepherds over his people that will help to develop the fruit of the Spirit in them (verse 27). So many ministers are just taking from the people and not giving back. They just want to preach a little sermonette on Sunday, shake their hands at the end of the service, and collect their tithes. They just see it as a business to take from the people. When they want more money they bring in a heavy hitter who majors in making people cry and raising money. Sadly, for some ministers, ministry is just a scam to fleece people and making them smile as they pick their pocket. These kinds of pastors are opening themselves up to the judgment of God.

In Ezekiel 37, God shows Ezekiel the valley of dry bones. These are the sheep that have been neglected by his pastors. God is going to raise up pastors and prophets to speak into their lives and they will rise up as a great army (verse 10). He said they have no hope (verse 11–13) but that he will bring them into their purpose (verse 14). You can see why God is bringing judgment during this month: what kind of a father would let his children be mistreated, taken advantage of, and walk around aimlessly without purpose? Most earthly fathers would not stand idly by, and neither will our heavenly Father. They don't realize that a true minister treats the people that God brought to them as children of God. True ministers allow the Father to speak through them into the lives of his people.

God also mentions in Zechariah 8:19 that this tenth month is also a time of great joy and feasting. For those who want to conform to the image of Jesus above anything, they will escape God's judgment during this time. For them, this is a great time to rejoice in their Father's approval and feast on his love.

Let's summarize the importance of the tenth month as a whole:

1. A time of great joy and feasting for some of God's people.

A summary of the importance of specific days during the tenth month:

1. Tenth Day and Twelfth Day - A time of great judgment by God on some of his people because of idolatry and covetousness. A time of judgment on some of God's pastors because of the mistreatment of his children. Replacement of the false pastors with those who have the heart of David.

There are some truths about the number ten in the Word that generally apply to this month. The number ten in the Word means that in this tenth month in particular, God wants to cut the devil off from the area of your life that he is attacking.

This meaning of the number ten in the Word is evident in Revelation 2:10: "You shall have tribulation ten days." In this scripture, God is saying that all the devil has is ten days and then he is cut off. You need to apply this number to your life on a frequent basis and cut the devil off by saying the number ten to him, by faith. His power will be broken as you use the number ten with faith. In this tenth month, whatever the devil was doing to you is cut off. You could be delivered from that habit that was separating you from God. You are now delivered from those people who were interfering with your walk with God. In 1 Samuel 17:18, Jesse tells David to take ten cheeses and ten loaves of bread to his brothers. When his father says this, David knows the battle was over and that the enemy would be cut off by God. Do you realize that God is doing the same thing to you, cutting off the devil from that area of your life where he is attacking?

In Genesis 1:4, God mentions that he divided the light from darkness. This is the effect of the number ten working in your life (i.e. the darkness is separated from your life)! In Genesis 24:22, the servant of Abraham gives Rebekah two bracelets weighing ten shekels of gold. This is God showing that the search for a bride for Isaac is over and she was the one.

God also confirms this truth in Genesis 45:23 as Joseph sends ten asses with good things for Jacob as well as ten asses loaded with corn. This is also signifying that the famine is over for Jacob and his family.

In Genesis 31:7, Jacob mentions that Laban changed his wages ten times. God is speaking here that the control that Laban had on Jacob and his wives is cut off once and for all. This is evident when God tells Laban not to touch Jacob in verse 24, not to harm him. He is delivered from Laban's dishonesty and tricks. From this time on Jacob spoils Laban, by getting his best cattle. You too can stop the devil from stealing your wages and get God's best for you by using the number ten as a mighty weapon, especially during this tenth month!

Praise him for the number ten in your life. Be encouraged when God shows this number to you during a trial. He is telling you that the devil is cut off from that area of your life he is attacking.

Remember, this tenth month is not the only time that God can cut the devil off from your life, but it is God's most anointed time to do so.

ELEVENTH MONTH

Shevat (Jan.-Feb.)

In Zechariah 1:7–13, the Word of the Lord comes on the twenty-fourth day of the eleventh month and he says that he will now extend mercy to his people that he had to punish previously through their enemies. This is a great promise for those who have strayed.

In 2:7–9, God says he sends deliverance and brings restitution against our enemies as he comes on the scene (verse 10). During this time of the month God also says in chapter 3 that he brings an anointing to clean us up (verse 4), crowns us with new authority (verse 5), and brings us into purpose (verse 7). He assures during this time also that it is only by his power that we can go into purpose (4:6), that any mountain in our way will become a plain (verse 7), that he is causing us to stand in our purpose (verse 14), and that he is sending more people to help us build (6:15). This is truly an exciting time of the month.

In Deuteronomy 1:3–8, on the first day of the eleventh month, Moses encourages the people to go in and possess the land God gave them and not to be fearful (verse 21). God encourages us the same way during this time. He also speaks a blessing on them to multiply like the stars of the sky (verse 10) and that God would make them a thousand times greater than they were (verse 11). During this time of the month God speaks the same blessings, just receive. I claim it for you now in Jesus' name.

Let's summarize the importance of specific days during the eleventh month:

1. First Day - God also encourages us to go into and possess our purpose or inheritance and speaks a multiplication blessing into our lives.

2. Twenty Fourth Day - God really pours out to his people with mercy, deliverance, restitution against their enemies, cleansing, new authority, bringing more builders to help, etc.

There is a general anointing on this eleventh month for God to confirm how close you are to your promotion, especially if you are going through a trial. During this eleventh month, you may feel a little nervous. God is telling you how close you may be to your new spiritual level. What's happening is that your body is getting used to the new spiritual level and you may feel a little uncomfortable.

For example, if you were told on your job on a Friday, that Monday you would be promoted and start a new position, you would be all right until Sunday night. You may start to feel a little nervous about your new duties. This is similar to a new level or promotion. During this month, where you are so close to starting your new assignment for God, you may feel a little nervous even though you have been promoted. You can't do the assignment without God.

A perfect example of this is 2 Chronicles 20, where Jehoshaphat fears when he is surrounded by the enemy (verse 3). He realizes, and you will too, that the battle is

God's (verse 15). God is ready to promote Jehoshaphat by wiping out his enemies and giving him their spoils which took three days to gather (verse 22–25).

When God promotes, he does more and you do less. At every new level, God shows us how powerful he really is as he does so much for us and in us. He is able to do so much in us and through us at this new level because only he could have taken you through a trial to get you to this point. At this stage in our walk with Jesus, we truly decrease as he increases.

The use of the number eleven in the Word by the Holy Spirit backs up the belief that the new level or promotion is at hand. In Genesis chapter 45 Joseph reveals himself to his eleven brothers and they are about to be promoted. Because of Joseph's position and authority in Egypt, they and the rest of their relatives get choice land, and are now being taken care of by Joseph. They don't have to be concerned about the famine any more. They now have abundance. During this eleventh month you are getting ready for the abundance that is at the end of a particular trial. So as you are approaching the end of a trial and you are feeling humbled and a little nervous, you are at the door of your new level or promotion, which could happen in the next month (twelfth).

TWELFTH MONTH

Adar (Feb.-Mar.)

In Jeremiah 52:31, the Word records that Evilmerodach, king of Babylon, releases Jehoiachin, king of Judah, from prison. This takes place on the twenty-fifth day of the twelfth month. Not only does he release him, but sets him up in his kingdom above his leaders. This enemy king takes care of his needs the rest of his life. This is a move of deliverance by God and should encourage anyone who needs to be delivered from the prison they are in. Receive your deliverance, as God's anointing to set you free is freely flowing, especially at this time of the month.

This is also a time of God's judgment coming forth; in Ezekiel 32:1–12, God tells the Pharaoh of Egypt on the first day of the twelfth month that he is going to bring destruction on him and the rest of the Egyptians. He says that his destruction would be so fierce that other nations will be terribly afraid for their own lives when they see Egypt's destruction at his hands.

God is not somebody to fool around with or someone to lean too heavily on his grace. He is also a God of justice, a God of vengeance, even though he is also a God of love. He will take vengeance on our enemies if they push him too far. They may seem to be winning and not relenting in their attacks on you, but take strength in the fact that God is on your side.

During this month on the fourteenth and fifteenth

days, the feast of Purim occurs. Purim is a wonderful feast that commemorates the deliverance of God's people from the wicked plans of Haman (Satan). God will always be ready to deliver his people and this time of the year is a wonderful time to claim and receive it.

Let's summarize the importance of specific days during the twelfth month:

1. The First Day of the month- Another time of God's judgment on our enemies.

2. The Fourteenth, Fifteenth and Twenty-Fifth Day- Other times for great deliverance by God.

The twelfth month as a whole is an excellent time for God to complete your promotion or new level he was preparing you for during the year but especially in the eleventh month. He can do this at any time in the twelfth month. Of course he can promote at any time of the year, but there is an anointing on this month especially to do so.

THIRTEENTH MONTH

(FEB-MAR)

These feasts or seasons I have discussed in this book are celebrated on the same day of the Hebrew calendar every year, but the Hebrew year is not the same length as a solar year on the Gregorian calendar used by most of the western world. As a result, the dates of these seasons change on the Gregorian calendar.

The Hebrew calendar is based on the rotation of the Earth about its axis (a day), the revolution of the moon about the Earth (about 29 1/2 days), and the revolution of the Earth about the sun (about 365 1/4 days, or 12.4 lunar months). The Hebrew calendar coordinates these three facts, and as a result, some years on the Hebrew calendar have thirteen months, which is considered a leap year. The Gregorian calendar does not (the length of the months has been arbitrarily set at 28, 30, or 31 days).

The following charts show the dates of God's appointed feasts both on the Hebrew calendar and the Gregorian calendar up to the year 2012. In a leap year, the thirteenth month is called Adar 2, and the twelfth month is called Adar 1. The additional month (Adar I) is inserted before the regular month of Adar (which is Adar II in a leap year). In a non-leap year, the twelfth month is called simply Adar. In certain years, the last day of Hanukkah is Tevet 3 as opposed to Tevet 2. Also, the feast of Purim will occur in Adar 2 in a leap year.

My charts take these facts into consideration. The same dates and blessings associated with the twelfth month are applicable here in this thirteenth month.

Here is the list of the Hebrew (our) months of the year again to help you:

First Month	Nisan	Mar-Apr.
Second Month	Iyar	Apr-May
Third Month	Sivan	May-June
Fourth Month	Tammuz	June-July
Fifth Month	Av	July-Aug.
Sixth Month	Elul	Aug-Sept.
Seventh Month	Tishrei	Sept.-Oct.
Eight Month	Cheshvan	Oct.-Nov.
Ninth Month	Kislev	Nov.-Dec.
Tenth Month	Tevet	Dec.- Jan.
Eleventh Month	Shevat	Jan.- Feb.
Twelfth Month	Adar	Feb.-Mar.
*Thirteenth Month	Adar 2	Mar-Apr.

* As I mentioned, only in a leap year is there a thirteenth month.

The following is a compilation of the particular month blessing periods up to an including the year 2012. If there is a particular day of the month (or the month as a whole) where there is a special anointing to bring about certain blessings, which you have learned from reading my book you can figure which day it is on the Gregorian calendar by going to www.hebcal.com/hebcal/. Again, when you are on this website please check off "show Hebrew date for entire date range" under "Other Options." Please refer to the chart above in researching the month of interest you desire to see from the word and go to a particular day in that month on this Hebrew calendar. Remember that the twenty four hour period of time which includes day and night runs from evening to evening.

Here is an example from the month of March in 2010 to help you in locating a particular day on the Gregorian calendar from a Hebrew date in the word: If you want to see which day on the Gregorian calendar Nisan 1 falls on you can see from this chart. Nisan 1 or the first day of the first month of the year starts on evening March 15 and ends on evening March 16.

March 2010

Sunday	Monday	Tuesday	Wednesday	Thursday	Friday	Saturday
	1 15th of Adar, 5770	2 16th of Adar, 5770	3 17th of Adar, 5770	4 18th of Adar, 5770	5 19th of Adar, 5770	6 20th of Adar, 5770
7 21st of Adar, 5770	8 22nd of Adar, 5770	9 23rd of Adar, 5770	10 24th of Adar, 5770	11 25th of Adar, 5770	12 26th of Adar, 5770	13 27th of Adar, 5770
14 28th of Adar, 5770	15 29th of Adar, 5770	16 1st of Nisan, 5770 X	17 2nd of Nisan, 5770	18 3rd of Nisan, 5770	19 4th of Nisan, 5770	20 5th of Nisan, 5770
21 6th of Nisan, 5770	22 7th of Nisan, 5770	23 8th of Nisan, 5770	24 9th of Nisan, 5770	25 10th of Nisan, 5770	26 11th of Nisan, 5770	27 12th of Nisan, 5770
28 13th of Nisan, 5770	29 14th of Nisan, 5770	30 15th of Nisan, 5770	31 16th of Nisan, 5770			

GOD'S MONTHLY
BLESSING PERIODS

2010

		Evening	Evening
1st	Month Nisan	Mar. 15	Apr. 14
2nd	Month Iyar	Apr. 14	May 13
3rd	Month Sivan	May 13	June 12
4th	Month Tammuz	June 12	July 11
5th	Month Av	July 11	Aug. 10
6th	Month Elul	Aug. 10	Sept. 8
7th	Month Tishrei	Sept. 8	Oct. 8
8th.	Month. Cheshvan	Oct. 8	Nov. 7
9th	Month Kislev	Nov. 7	Dec. 7
10th	Month Tevet	Dec. 7	Jan. 5 (2011)
11th	Month Shevat	Jan. 5	Feb. 4
12th	Month Adar	Feb. 4	Mar. 6
13th	Month * Adar 2	Mar. 6	Apr. 4

* The blessings associated with the twelfth month are equally applicable to the thirteenth month. God is in his infinite wisdom gives us another month in a leap year to enjoy the blessings associated with the prior month.

GOD'S MONTHLY BLESSING PERIODS

2011

		Evening	Evening
1st	Month Nisan	Apr. 4	May 4
2nd	Month Iyar	May 4	June 2
3rd	Month Sivan	June 2	July 2
4th	Month Tammuz	July 2	July 31
5th	Month Av	July 31	Aug. 30
6th	Month Elul	Aug. 30	Sept. 28
7th	Month Tishrei	Sept. 28	Oct. 28
8th	Month. Cheshvan	Oct. 28	Nov. 26
9th	Month Kislev	Nov. 26	Dec. 26
10th	Month Tevet	Dec. 26	Jan. 24 (2012)
11th	Month Shevat	Jan. 24	Feb. 23
12th	Month Adar	Feb. 23	Mar. 23

GOD'S MONTHLY
BLESSING PERIODS

2012

		Evening	Evening
1st	Month Nisan	Mar. 23	Apr. 22
2nd	Month Iyar	Apr. 22	May 21
3rd	Month Sivan	May 21	June 20
4th	Month Tammuz	June 20	July 19
5th	Month Av	July 19	Aug. .18
6th	Month Elul	Aug. 18	Sept. 16
7th	Month Tishrei	Sept. 16	Oct. 16
8th	Month. Cheshvan	Oct. 16	Nov. 14
9th	Month Kislev	Nov. 14	Dec. 13
10th	Month Tevet	Dec. 13	Jan. 11 (2013)
11th	Month Shevat	Jan. 11	Feb. 10
12th	Month Adar	Feb. 10	Mar. 11

For God's monthly blessing periods past 2012, please go to www.henrywalker.org and click on "Biblical Calendar."

The following charts show the dates of God's appointed feasts both on the Hebrew calendar and the Gregorian calendar up to the year 2012.

GOD'S APPOINTED TIMES

2010

Hebrew Month Evening to Evening

1.	Nisan 1–Biblical New Year–	Mar. 15	Mar. 16
2.	Nisan 14–Passover–	Mar. 28	Mar. 29
3.	Nisan 15–21–Unleavened Bread–	Mar. 29	Apr. 5
4.	Nisan 16-Sivan 6–Firstfruits	Mar. 30	May 18
5.	Sivan 6–Pentecost	May 18	May 19
6.	Elul 1–Tishri 10–Teshuvah	Aug. 10	Sept. 17
7.	Tishri 1, 2–Rosh HaShannah–Civil New Year	Sept. 8	Sept. 10
8.	Tishri 10–Yon Kippur (Day of Atonement)	Sept. 17	Sept. 18
9.	Tishri 15–21–Tabernacles	Sept. 22	Sept. 30
10.	Kislev 25–Tevet 2–Hanukkah	Dec. 1	Dec. 9
11.	(Adar 2) - 14, 15–Purim (2011)	Mar. 19	Mar. 21
12.	Weekly Blessing Time -Sabbath and Sunday		

GOD'S APPOINTED TIMES

2011

Hebrew Month Evening to Evening

1. Nisan 1–Biblical New Year–	Apr. 4	Apr. 5
2. Nisan 14–Passover–	Apr. 17	Apr. 18
3. Nisan 15–21–Unleavened Bread–	Apr. 18	Apr. 25
4. Nisan 16-Sivan 6–Firstfruits	Apr. 19	June. 7
5. Sivan 6–Pentecost	June. 7	June. 8
6. Elul 1–Tishri 10–Teshuvah	Aug. 30	Oct. 7
7. Tishri 1, 2–Rosh HaShannah–Civil New Year	Sept. 28	Sept. 30
8. Tishri 10–Yon Kippur (Day of Atonement)	Oct. 7	Oct. 8
9. Tishri 15–21–Tabernacles	Oct. 12	Oct. 20
10. Kislev 25–Tevet 2–Hanukkah	Dec. 20	Dec. 28
11. Adar 14, 15–Purim (2012)	Mar. 7	Mar. 9
12. Weekly Blessing Time -Sabbath and Sunday		

GOD'S APPOINTED TIMES

2012

Hebrew Month Evening to Evening

1.	Nisan 1–Biblical New Year–	Mar. 23	Mar. 24
2.	Nisan 14–Passover–	Apr. 5	Apr. 6
3.	Nisan 15–21–Unleavened Bread–	Apr. 6	Apr. 13
4.	Nisan 17-Sivan 6–Firstfruits	Apr. 7	May 26
5.	Sivan 6–Pentecost	May 26	May 27
6.	Elul 1–Tishri 10–Teshuvah	Aug. 18	Sept. 25
7.	Tishri 1, 2–Rosh HaShannah–Civil New Year	Sept. 16	Sept. 18
8.	Tishri 10–Yon Kippur (Day of Atonement)	Sept. 25	Sept. 26
9.	Tishri 15–21–Tabernacles	Sept. 30	Oct. 8
10.	Kislev 25–Tevet 3–Hanukkah *	Dec. 8	Dec. 16
11.	Adar 14, 15–Purim (2013)	Feb. 23	Feb. 25
12.	Weekly Blessing Time -Sabbath and Sunday		

*Because of Hebrew calendar adjustments, Hanukkah ends on Tevet 3

For God's appointed times past 2012, please go to www.henrywalker.org and click on "Biblical Calendar."

CONCLUSION

I pray that you enjoyed this book, and I also pray that you have a deeper awareness of God's special blessing times on an hourly, daily, and monthly basis. You can also search the Word for other periods of time such as number of days, months, or years, and see if they are applicable to your situation.

You may see in the Word that Joshua marched around Jericho for seven days and the walls came down. You may get a witness in your spirit that your Jericho will come down in seven days. Your relatives may have had problems in the family for forty years. You may see in the Word that the Israelites were in the wilderness for forty years, but Joshua, Caleb, and the children came out. You can claim that the family wilderness is over, if God puts this in your spirit. Not everybody can claim these time period promises unless God speaks to their spirit. It is just a matter of one seeking the Holy Spirit and seeing if God wants to move in these time frames. It won't be for everybody, but it could be a blessing time frame for someone.

The promises mentioned in this book at hourly, daily, and monthly time periods are available for anybody who will seek Jesus and be prepared. I am sure your walk with Jesus will never be the same as you prepare for these blessing times. As I mentioned earlier, if you don't receive the blessing that you are expecting at a certain period of time, maybe God is trying to make some adjustments in your life, in order for you to receive. Just listen to the Holy Spirit and believe to receive at the next time period. Your life will never be the same as you now aware of the Lord's blessing time periods and position yourself to receive.